J

THE EPISTLES OF
JOHN

Devotional
Studies on
LIVING CONFIDENTLY

THE EPISTLES OF
JOHN

Devotional
Studies on
LIVING CONFIDENTLY

by

J. ALLEN BLAIR

LOIZEAUX BROTHERS

Neptune, New Jersey

FIRST EDITION, JUNE 1982

Library of Congress Cataloging in Publication Data

Blair, J. Allen, 1913—
    The Epistles of John.

    1. Bible.   N.T.   Epistles of John—Commentaries.
I. Bible.   N.T.   Epistles of John.   English.   1982.
II. Title.
BS2805.3.B56   227'.9407   82-15196
ISBN 0-87213-028-2   AACR2

PRINTED IN THE UNITED STATES OF AMERICA

*Dedicated
to
All the Glad Tidings Staff
and Board Members
who have shared
their time and talents
so generously
in our radio and literature outreach*

CONTENTS

Living Confidently

Chapter 4

Chapter 5

THE SECOND EPISTLE OF JOHN

THE THIRD EPISTLE OF JOHN

INTRODUCTION

Would you experience the joy of "living confidently," with the assurance of being prepared to meet God? Then lay hold of the contents of the Epistles of John. Its writer says, "These things have I written unto you that believe on the name of the Son of God; that ye may know that ye have eternal life" (1 John 5:13). There is no need for anyone to *hope* he is saved, for he may *know*. Read this brief Epistle with this thought in mind and notice how clearly the truth unfolds.

Who wrote First John? It is somewhat like the Epistle to the Hebrews in that the writer does not disclose his identity. The authorship seems obvious, however, because of the unusual style which is easily recognized as that of John, the son of Zebedee. The thoughts, phrases, and spiritual depth are much like those contained in the Gospel written by the same author.

When was First John written? John's writings were the final ones given by God. It has been thought that several of Paul's Epistles were the last portions given. But Paul had departed to glory some twenty years before John wrote his Gospel. John was the last surviving member of the apostolic band and wrote his first Epistle about 90 A.D. From the available evidence, it would seem that the book of the Revelation, written by John, was the last inspired book the Lord gave.

To whom was the Epistle written? While some books of the Bible are addressed to particular individuals or assemblies, First John seems to be for all true believers in general: "You that believe on the name of the Son of God" (1 John 5:13). This is not to suggest that other books of the Bible which are addressed to specific persons are not for the entire body of Christ. Though all Scripture may not be written *to us* directly, it is all *for us* generally. Paul makes this clear in 2 Timothy 3:16-17: "All scripture is given by inspiration of God, and is profitable . . . That the man of God may be perfect, thoroughly furnished unto all good works."

The unique feature of First John is that it is not only *for us*, but *to us*. Thus, the true believer may eat and drink of the spiritual feast the Holy Spirit has made available in this marvelous Epistle.

Why was the Epistle written? There seem to be several reasons, the most important being that those who have believed on Christ might possess the assurance of salvation. The apostle wrote his Gospel for unbelievers that they might *believe* and be saved. His first Epistle was written that those who have believed might *know* that they are saved. Twenty-six times the word "know" is used in the first Epistle.

During its short history, the infant Church had gone through many storms. Much of the distress was the result of false teaching. Confused and perplexed, some believers were doubting their salvation. John assured them that, though believers may not know all things, there are certain absolutes which cannot be questioned, one of which is, "he that hath the Son hath life" (1 John 5:12). The apostle was vitally concerned that all believers possess this unquestionable confidence.

In addition to emphasizing the believer's assurance, John launched an attack on the false teaching that had found its way into the church. At the time, the Gnostics were denying the humanity of Christ. This is probably why little is said about Christ's deity in First John. Just the opposite was the case in John's Gospel, where Christ is presented as the Son of God. In the first Epistle, Christ's deity is taken for granted, while His perfect humanity is presented in convincing clarity.

Another major concern of the apostle in his first Epistle is the much-needed grace of love in the hearts of believers. The word "love" is used forty-six times. With the growth and expansion of the church came personality clashes, jealousy, and bitterness. Years before, Paul had written the memorable 1 Corinthians 13. But with discord and division disrupting the harmony of the assemblies, John, the apostle of love, was divinely directed to accentuate the message of old that "He that loveth not knoweth not God; for God is love" (1 John 4:8).

There is also an emphasis on personal purity. Though the word "light" is used only six times, the fact is stressed that "God is light" (1 John 1:5) and those who follow Him should "walk in the light" (1 John 1:7). John was provoked with the teaching that, though one was saved, he could continue in sin and still be a child of God. The first Epistle makes it clear that such teaching was erroneous.

As we begin the study of this challenging yet comforting portion of God's Word, let us face the reality of our own spiritual condition by giving heed to 2 Corinthians 13:5, "Examine yourselves, whether ye be in the faith; prove your own selves." Do we really know the Lord or do we only "think" we know Him? .Though the first Epistle of John is written primarily to believers, the apostle is aware of the many who "think" they are believers but have never had a real heart transformation. Consequently, the message of salvation appears throughout. John does not want anyone to miss the truth. If you have any doubts about your relationship to the Lord, get things settled once and for all; "Believe on the Lord Jesus Christ, and thou shalt be saved" (Acts 16:31).

J. ALLEN BLAIR

THE FIRST EPISTLE
OF JOHN

1

DERIVATION

That which was from the beginning, which we have heard, which we have seen with our eyes, which we have looked upon, and our hands have handled, of the Word of life; (For the life was manifested, and we have seen it, and bear witness, and shew unto you that eternal life, which was with the Father, and was manifested unto us.) (1 John 1:1-2).

In all probability, John had been released from his imprisonment on the Isle of Patmos and was residing in Ephesus, where he wrote this Epistle. His first statement is extremely meaningful. As the elder statesman of believers, he had seen the diabolical effects of unbelief and heresy in the church. Due to the false teachers, much misunderstanding had resulted, especially among the young believers. Frequently the question was heard, "What shall we believe?"

There is only one message to believe: "That which was from the beginning" (1:1). This is the message that proclaims Christ and all that pertains to Him: His miraculous birth, His spotless life, His divine power, His substitutionary death, and His glorious resurrection. This is what one must believe if he is to experience eternal life and all of its benefits. God's message must never be changed. While some believers are "tossed to

13

and fro, and carried about with every wind of doctrine, by the sleight of men, and cunning craftiness" (Ephesians 4:14), those who would experience peace, blessing, and assurance must hold to "that which was from the beginning."

"The beginning" spoken of here is the same time referred to in John's Gospel: "In the beginning was the Word, and the Word was with God, and the Word was God. The same was in the beginning with God" (John 1:1-2). This is the beginning of creation, not the beginning of Christ, for He, the Father, and the Holy Spirit are without beginning. When God's creation began, Christ, with all of His attributes, was existent. In fact, the creation we enjoy is the work of the Son of God who existed eternally before the universe was created.

Thus, what we believe, as followers of Christ, is not new, or even several hundred years old. It is the age-old message of truth which had its derivation in "the beginning." It will continue to exist even after the heavens and the earth pass away.

If you are wondering what to believe amidst all the religions with their various teachings and philosophies, believe "that which was from the beginning." This message has never changed or needed revision. It is the eternal truth of God as revealed and manifested through Jesus, God's Son.

The Apostle Paul had something to say about this message in his valuable treatise on the resurrection: "Moreover, brethren, I declare unto you the gospel which I preached unto you, which also ye have received, and wherein ye stand; By which also ye are saved, if ye keep in memory what I have preached unto you, unless ye have believed in vain. For I delivered unto you first of all that which I also received, how that Christ died for our sins according to the scriptures; And that He was buried, and that He rose again the third day according to the scriptures" (1 Corinthians 15:1-4). Nothing could be clearer; we "are saved" by believing in the crucified and resurrected Christ.

One may believe that Jesus was simply a good man, while attempting to pattern his life after Christ's example. Doubtless this will tend to lift one toward Heaven, but only as he submits to the Son of God as Saviour and Lord will he be allowed to enter Heaven. We know this because of "that which was from the beginning." This is not a new discovery; the message is as old as the creation of the world. It is the profound truth that is revealed in God's Word from Genesis to Revelation.

"That which was from the beginning" is the message every human in the world needs to hear, for it is the message that provides deliverance from all the frustrations and fears of life resulting from the mixed up and chaotic world in which we live. How consoling is the truth that "if the Son therefore shall make you free, ye shall be free indeed" (John 8:36). It is the message that molds families together and keeps couples from the divorce court as they submit "one to another in the fear of God" (Ephesians 5:21). It is the message that assures the survival of the nations that heed it and believe it. The penalty is certain for those who fail to believe it: "The wicked shall be turned into hell, and all the nations that forget God" (Psalm 9:17). It is the message that can stabilize our educational system and train our youth for respectability and worthwhile endeavors, for "the fear of the LORD is the beginning of wisdom: and the knowledge of the holy is understanding" (Proverbs 9:10). It is the message that can solve the economic problems of the world, enabling us to recognize where the true values of life really are. It will help us to "beware of covetousness," understanding that "a man's life consisteth not in the abundance of the things which he possesseth" (Luke 12:15). It is the message that could bring warmth and value to the churches proclaiming the social gospel which is no gospel at all. God warns, "Beware of false prophets, which come to you in sheep's clothing, but inwardly they are ravening wolves" (Matthew 7:15). It is the message that could change the course of our civilization from its downward path of destruction to one of prosperity and blessing. It is axiomatic that "righteousness exalteth a nation: but sin is a reproach to any people" (Proverbs 14:34).

Of course, to be effective, this message must be believed. To be believed, Christ must be received. To receive Christ is to invite Him into the life as Saviour and Lord. Nothing else will do. There are no substitutes.

A lady was in the hospital, seriously ill. A family member sent for her minister to come and give her Communion. He came, but his visit gave her no peace. After he left, she said to the patient in the next bed, "I thought it would have done me more good." The patient replied, "You don't want *it*. You want *Him*." It is Christ we need; only as we heed the truth "which was from the beginning" can we know life, peace, and happiness.

"That which was from the beginning" consisted not only of fundamental truths, but of a Person. This he substantiated not by mere hearsay, but by actual experience: "We have heard . . . we have seen . . . we have looked upon . . . and our hands have handled, of the Word of life."

Doubtless this was written to refute the teachings of a group in the church known as Gnostics. The Gnostics were divided among the Docetics and the Cerinthians. The errors they taught dealt primarily with the person of the Lord Jesus. The Docetic Gnostics denied the humanity of Christ, saying that He did not have an actual body; He only seemed to have a body. The Cerinthian Gnostics denied the virgin birth, teaching that Jesus was born of human parents, but at His baptism Christ descended upon Him in the form of a dove, at which time He began to do the works of the Father until the cross, when the Christ departed again from Jesus.

Directed by the Holy Spirit, the apostle sought to combat these errors in his first Epistle. His initial argument is one that cannot be disproved easily, that of a personal relationship and experience. John "heard" Christ speak, not once, but innumerable times. Much of what he heard has been recorded for our benefit in the fourth Gospel.

Considering the length of the Gospel with all it contains about what Christ spoke and taught, one wonders how anyone could possibly retain so much to write at a much later date. We cannot overlook divine inspiration. There is no question about John's listening to the Son of God with intensity. But what he wrote involved more than this. God, the Holy Spirit, brought back to his mind the things the apostle heard and enabled him to record them with accuracy.

Not only was it by his auditory nerves that John was made aware of the fact of Christ's humanity, but through his sense of vision, as well. He heard Christ speak many, many times, and he also saw Him. What John wrote was not the result of dreams or hallucinations. He actually saw the body of the Lord Jesus Christ.

The word used for "seeing" embodies more than a visual impression; it has to do with a mental perception.

John thoroughly understood what he saw. He realized without question that he looked upon the Son of God.

In addition to hearing and sight, John had physical contact with Christ, having touched His actual body. What greater proof does one need?

Recall how Thomas laughed at the report he received from the other disciples of the resurrected Christ. Boldly he affirmed, "Except I shall see in His hands the print of the nails, and put my finger into the print of the nails, and thrust my hand into His side, I will not believe" (John 20:25). Eight days later, as Christ appeared to him in the presence of the other disciples, he was invited by our Lord to reach out his hand and touch the scars. But for Thomas, this was not necessary; seeing was believing; he needed nothing beyond this. Convinced, he cried out, "My Lord and my God" (John 20:28).

John went further than Thomas. Not only did he hear and see Christ, he touched Him. There was no question in the apostle's mind about the Son of God being an actual human when He was on this earth.

What is so important about the humanity of Christ? Is it not enough that He is the Son of God? The humanity of Christ is of extreme importance to the child of God. Consider the consoling truths of Hebrews 4:15-16: "For we have not an high priest which cannot be touched with the feeling of our infirmities; but was in all points tempted like as we are, yet without sin. Let us therefore come boldly unto the throne of grace, that we may obtain mercy, and find grace to help in time of need." Because of His humanity, our Lord understands all about temptation. We have been tempted and have yielded many times. Always, when Christ faced temptation, He emerged victorious. As believers, we too can be victorious. As we unload our cares upon

Him and trust Him for His power, we can be "more than conquerors through Him" (Romans 8:37).

John described the One he was writing about as "the Word of life." In his Gospel, he presented Christ as "the Word": "In the beginning was the Word, and the Word was with God, and the Word was God . . . . And the Word was made flesh, and dwelt among us, (and we beheld His glory, the glory as of the only begotten of the Father,) full of grace and truth" (John 1:1,14). John also revealed that not only is Christ "the Word," He is the "life": "In Him was life; and the life was the light of men" (John 1:4). In his first Epistle, he combined the two expressions, presenting Christ as the "Word of life."

Probably no designation could describe Christ better than "Word of life." Not only does He give life to those who believe, but He lives His life through them. Many Christians struggle to live "a good Christian life." What they need to realize is that victory over sin is not something achieved, but something received. It is experienced through complete dependence on the life of Christ within. The same Lord who purchased our forgiveness on the cross gives the victory we cannot accomplish ourselves, but receive by faith as we rely on Christ. Only as we allow Him to live in and through us can we possibly know victory and blessing in the Christian life.

The secret of Christian victory is not found in our fleshly efforts but in the enabling power of Jesus Christ. This truth is expressed so well by Paul in Galatians 2:20, "I am crucified with Christ: nevertheless I live; yet not I, but Christ liveth in me: and the life which I now live in the flesh I live by the faith of the Son of God, who loved me, and gave Himself for me."

Are you allowing Christ, the Word of life, to live through you or are you attempting to do "works of righteousness" in your own strength? Let Him do it. Only He can, for He is "the Word of life."

"The life was manifested, and we have seen it." God is the only source of eternal life. In His mercy, He "manifested," that is, made this life available to everyone through His Son. This great fact was made known to the world at the incarnation when "the Word was made flesh, and dwelt among us" (John 1:14).

In writing of this life, John shared his personal experience: "We have seen it." It should be noted that this is more than the visual recognition as in verse 1. The thought expressed is not that of seeing with the eye but rather an experience of the heart, that Christ be appropriated personally as Lord. This became a reality in the apostle's life. When he saw Christ, by believing he experienced eternal life. It became his possession.

There are many tens of thousands in our present day who are familiar with Christ and His sacrifice for sin, yet have not "seen" Him in a personal experience. Often their lives are empty, without peace or pleasure.

Those who have truly "seen" Christ in a new-life experience will show their gratitude by a ready response. "We have seen it, and bear witness, and shew unto you that eternal life, which was with the Father, and was manifested unto us." After one has "seen" Christ, he should "bear witness," and show others the "eternal life" he has experienced. It is hard to understand how anyone who has entered into a personal relationship with the One who was identical "with the Father" in His deity and authority can overlook his obligation to tell others about Him.

In the fourth chapter of John's Gospel, we are told of one of the great women in the New Testament. She had come to draw water from the well. There she met

Christ who spoke to her about the water of life. Profoundly interested, she drank of the water of life and experienced a new life through Christ. Overjoyed, she left her waterpot and hastily returned to the city shouting, "Come, see a man, which told me all things that ever I did: is not this the Christ?" (John 4:29)

This woman saw, and then bore witness. "And many of the Samaritans of that city believed on Him for the saying of the woman, which testified, He told me all that ever I did" (John 4:39). We are not told how many believed as the result of this woman's faithful testimony, but there must have been a great number. The Lord honors the witness of His people.

Considering the countless number of new religious movements and cults that are springing up everywhere, it is more necessary than ever that God's people witness. Someone has suggested that there are at least two thousand new religious groups in the United States alone. Most of those who are being absorbed into false belief are teenagers and those in their twenties. While the enemy works, many believers sleep. Whether they be teenagers, young adults, or adults, everyone has spiritual needs that demand satisfaction. We, who are in Christ, know the only One who can honestly care for these spiritual needs, yet many who profess to be believers in Christ are either too busy or uninterested to be concerned about them. Thus, the counterfeits are moving in and Satan is blinding the minds of those who believe not, so that they are willing to believe a lie. If we have met the Lord, then we must witness and share Christ "while it is day: the night cometh, when no man can work" (John 9:4).

DECLARATION

That which we have seen and heard declare we unto you, that ye also may have fellowship with us: and truly our fellowship is with the Father, and with His Son Jesus Christ. And these things write we unto you, that your joy may be full (1 John 1:3-4).

John knew Christ personally. Having walked with Him, talked with Him, and worked with Him, he was motivated by a loving concern to declare to everyone possible "That which we have seen and heard."

The Christian life begins with "seeing" and "hearing" Christ. As one realizes who Christ is and humbly submits to His lordship, untold blessing will result. This is our only approach to eternal life. One may be a worthy church member, a helpful citizen, and in the eyes of his peers, a "good man," but until he receives salvation through the Son of God, spiritual truth will be meaningless to him. The moment he believes, the situation will change. That which was of little or no value suddenly becomes understandable and satisfying.

Paul tells of this transforming experience: "And you hath He quickened, who were dead in trespasses and sins; Wherein in time past ye walked according to the course of this world, according to the prince of the power of the air, the spirit that now worketh in the children of disobedience: Among whom also we all had our conversation in times past in the lusts of our flesh, fulfilling the desires of the flesh and of the mind; and were by nature the children of wrath, even as others. But God, who is rich in mercy, for His great love wherewith He loved us, Even when we were dead in sins, hath quickened us together with Christ, (by grace ye are saved)" (Ephesians 2:1-5).

When God saves a person, He goes to the source of the problem, the sinful heart. The repentant believer is changed by the power of God from the inside out.

Spurgeon used to say, "I have gone into my garden, and I have seen a great number of trees that have new branches which have been grafted into them, but I never yet saw a tree get a new heart. I have seen it get new bark, and many changes have happened to it, but it cannot change its heart."

No human can change his sinful heart. He may change his outward appearance, but his heart will remain the same. Unlike the tree, however, God can change a person's heart. When one trusts in Christ, God performs a mighty miracle and the heart of the repentant believer is transformed. The Lord is doing this constantly. Those who come to Him receive new motives, new desires, and new habits. Paul described this wonderful experience: "Therefore if any man be in Christ, he is a new creature: old things are passed away; behold, all things are become new" (2 Corinthians 5:17).

The new life is not merely for our enjoyment; it is to be shared with others. "That which we have seen and heard *declare* we unto you." God never intended that redemption be kept a secret. We are saved "from dead works to serve the living God" (Hebrews 9:14).

Those who are truly saved find a happiness such as they have never known before. But happiness is not the basic purpose for which we are saved; it is simply one of the by-products of salvation. We are saved to tell others, so they, too, might enter into the joys of everlasting life.

Who of us could receive an inheritance of a million dollars without sharing this news with our friends? Who would be unreasonable enough, after being cured of cancer, to refuse to reveal the name of the surgeon or remedy? Why is it that in the lesser experiences of life we are ready to talk for hours with gratitude and pleasure? Why do we not with the same enthusiasm share Christ with those who need Him? If "we have seen and heard" Christ, we should "declare" Him.

Was our salvation experience real? Were we really "plucked out of the burning" (Amos 4:11)? Or was ours merely an emotional stirring unrelated to the truth of God? It is easy for one to be stirred by the fervor of a zealous preacher in the midst of the excitement of the hour. Perhaps this is the reason why some professed believers do not last. Their profession was shallow and empty, not grounded in God's Word.

A worthy test of one's personal experience with the Lord is what happens afterward. Is there an earnest desire to bring others to the light? Is the heart burdened to lead friends and neighbors to Christ? God says, "Let the redeemed of the Lord say so" (Psalm 107:2). The believer should grasp every opportunity to "declare" Christ.

An evangelist from South America was conducting meetings in a Spanish church in New York City. Night after night, many of those who attended responded to the invitation to receive Christ. They were then directed to a room for counsel and instruction. On one occasion, the evangelist dealt with a young lady who was quite rebellious. As he talked with her, she expressed doubts as to why she even came forward. "You can't do anything for me," she said. "I am no good. I don't want to hear any more preaching."

With regret, the evangelist said, "Very well, but please let me pray with you; then you may go." As he prayed, his heart concern for this disillusioned young woman was so great that his voice broke and tears ran down his face. When he finished praying, as he wiped his eyes, he apologized with some embarrassment and said, "I've prayed. Now you may go." She stared at him strangely. "I will stay. You have wept for me. Now you may talk to me."

God assures us that if we have this kind of concern for the lost our efforts will not be in vain, for "He that goeth forth and weepeth, bearing precious seed, shall doubtless come again with rejoicing, bringing his sheaves with him" (Psalm 126:6).

One of the reasons why we should declare Christ is that the lost "may have fellowship with us." What an amazing fellowship this is! No club, organization, or lodge is comparable to the fellowship of believers in Christ Jesus. Like everyone else, Christians have their weaknesses. They get tired and fussy. They become nervous and irritable at times. But when they are Spirit-led and Spirit-controlled, their fellowship is unparalleled. As true friends, they are always ready and willing to help each other in any time of need. They pray for each other and share each other's burdens. There is a common bond of love among them as the result of their relationship through Christ. Because of His blood, shed at Calvary, Christians are one in Him, regardless of color, social status, or ability.

I was invited to conduct a Bible conference in a city I had never visited before. Before I left home, I heard that I had a relative there, whom I had never met. Upon arriving I contacted him, and the next night he and his wife and I went to dinner. After we got acquainted, I began to share Christ with them. But though they were delightful people, they had no interest in spiritual things. There was indifference to what I had to say about the Lord. Though we were blood relatives, we were miles apart in regard to that which I considered to be of greatest importance in life.

The following day, I was invited to lunch by one of the elders of the church where I was speaking. As we sat at the lunch table and talked, it took only minutes to realize that, even though we had not been acquainted before, because we were believers we had all things in common. The fellowship we enjoyed was priceless.

Upon returning to my hotel room, I thought of the evening before and the absence of fellowship with my own relative. Then I thought of my luncheon experience and the fellowship we enjoyed because of our relationship to Christ. Though we were not blood relatives, there was a sense in which we were related "by blood," for we were redeemed "with the precious blood of Christ, as of a lamb without blemish and without spot" (1 Peter 1:19).

The fellowship of believers is so unique and wonderful because "our fellowship is with the Father, and with His Son Jesus Christ." It is more than several people gathering together with a common interest to sing hymns and hear a sermon. For those who have not truly been born again, church attendance seems boring and dull. But to those who have truly come to know the Lord, worship with the people of God is most meaningful, for Christ is there. Whether it is in a mud hut in the South Pacific, a crude building in the hollow, or a cathedral on Fifth Avenue, if those worshiping are gathered in the name of Jesus Christ, He is there.

Our Lord said, "For where two or three are gathered

together in My name, there am I in the midst of them" (Matthew 18:20). Christ is not in one corner or the other. He is not in the pulpit. He is "in the midst." Because He is "in the midst," He is the same to every believer. He "is no respecter of persons" (Acts 10:34). All of us are loved equally. No child of God is any more important to Him than another. Whether it is the mill worker, the truck driver, the medical doctor, the chemist, the home-maker, the minister or whatever: we are all one in Christ. We enjoy fellowship with each other and with Jesus, our Lord. If you have been born of the Holy Spirit, John's words are meaningful to you: "Truly our fellowship is with the Father, and with His Son Jesus Christ."

Can one be absolutely certain that he is a part of this fellowship? Maybe you feel that you are, or hope that you are, but there are doubts at times. If you have truly received Christ, there need be no doubts. As you read God's Word and wait on Him, He will give you the confidence that you belong to Him.

A young man went to his minister for counsel as to how he could know when he was in love. "I go out with one girl, and then another; how will I know?" he asked. The minister replied emphatically, "Son, you will know."

The same is true of salvation. If you are wondering how you will know when you are saved, the answer is very simple: "You will know." When one turns to Christ sincerely and invites Him to become Lord of his life, God enters and the fellowship is established for eternity. The Holy Spirit will give an awareness of salvation and doubts will be banished. Even though the child of God may stumble and falter at times, Christ is always unchanging in His provision and care. He promises, "I will never leave thee, nor forsake thee" (Hebrews 13:5).

A saintly woman lay dying. Her loved ones were

gathered around her bed. Believing she was unable to hear, one of the relatives said quietly, "She's sinking fast." But the aged saint, half opening her eyes, shook her head feebly and whispered, "Oh, no, I am not sinking. You can't sink through a Rock."

Christ is the believer's Rock. If we know Him, we are secure. We may depend upon Him for everything. His sufficiency is adequate. We are His, and He is ours. At no time will He forget us because "truly our fellowship is with the Father, and with His Son Jesus Christ."

Are you enjoying this fellowship? Do you truly know Christ? I don't mean, do you know about him. Have you entered into a personal relationship with Him, so you can say, "Thank God I am in fellowship with Him. He is my Saviour and Lord." Don't dissipate the life God gave you. Live it the way He intended, in fellowship with Jesus, the Son of God. That is the happy life. Anything less than this is misery and defeat.

The apostle is concerned that believers do more than enter into fellowship with Christ. He wants them to enjoy the fullness of the blessing of being children of God: "And these things write we unto you, that your joy may be full." There are some believers who possess the assurance of salvation, yet are devoid of the fullness of joy which is theirs in Christ. The fact that some believers possess more joy than others is not that God is more favorable to some. It is a matter of submission to the Lord's control. The more yielded one is to Christ, the greater will be his enjoyment of the things of the Spirit.

This is not to suggest that he will be kept from toil or hardship. It is possible to live in extremely difficult circumstances, yet enjoy peace and confidence unknown to the unyielded life. Satan realizes this. Thus, after he loses one of his possessions to God through the redeeming power of Christ, he does all he can, by way of temptation, to upset the equilibrium of a well-balanced Christian life. This is why the Lord Jesus said, "Pray that ye enter not into temptation" (Luke 22:40). This does not mean that we are to pray that we shall not be tempted or tested. Not only is testing important, it is essential for Christian maturity. We should pray for strength through Christ to be victorious when tempted, for yielding to temptation will rob the believer of the treasure of God's joy.

God never intended that His people be of a sour or doleful disposition. He wants us to "rejoice with joy unspeakable and full of glory" (1 Peter 1:8). After speaking of the value of abiding in Him and all that is involved in this harmonious relationship, our Lord said to His own, "These things have I spoken unto you, that My joy might remain in you, and that your joy might be full" (John 15:11). Consequently, if you are not experiencing this fullness of joy, something is wrong—not with God, but with you. There may be some sin in your life— something which may appear to you to be insignificant. This could be the culprit. By the grace of God, claim victory through Christ and get it out of your life. Adverse feelings you have toward some of your friends will change. Dislike for your employment will disappear. Even disinterest in your daily routine will be remedied. Where there is resentment, there will be love. Where there is a lack of interest, there will be enthusiasm. Where there is rebellion, there will be submission. You will discover, as never before, that "the joy of the LORD is your strength" (Nehemiah 8:10). Life will take on a whole new dimension. Everyone around you will be aware that something tremendous has happened.

There are many Christians who have never entered

into this fullness of joy in Christ. They are saved but always struggling. Instead of living above their circumstances, they are bogged down by them. They are given to worry and frequent complaining. Occasionally they are joyful, but not very often. God would have us to understand that fullness of joy can be ours, regardless of our surroundings.

Paul and Silas were on their second missionary journey. While at Troas, Paul had a vision in which he saw a man in Macedonia praying that Paul might come and proclaim the truth. Confident that this was the leading of the Lord, Paul and Silas departed for Macedonia. Upon reaching Philippi, they were used of the Lord to lead a prominent businesswoman to Christ. Following her conversion, Lydia's whole household came to the Saviour. Next, Paul and Silas delivered from demonism a woman who had been used as a tool for fortune-telling by her wicked masters. Following her deliverance, she could no longer be used for selfish gain. Angered by this, the men had Paul and Silas arrested, accusing them falsely: "These men, being Jews, do exceedingly trouble our city, and teach customs, which are not lawful for us to receive, neither to observe, being Romans" (Acts 16:20-21). God's servants were judged to be guilty and after being severely beaten, they were imprisoned. But even worse, they were thought to be dangerous criminals and were placed in the inner prison with their feet locked in stocks, with no chance of escape. The situation could not have been worse for Paul and Silas. They could have pitied themselves, asking, "Where did we fail? Did we make a mistake in coming to Philippi?" But there was none of that. "At midnight Paul and Silas prayed, and sang praises unto God." In the midst of those horrible surroundings, with beaten and aching bodies, they rejoiced. How could they do it? Their joy was "full." They were yielded completely to Jesus Christ. He was in perfect control.

One reason John wrote his first Epistle was that God's people might know the fullness of His joy. If your joy is not full, Christ is ready to do something about it, if you are. Remember, all sin must be dealt with; only then can one know the blessing of the fullness of His joy.

DESCRIPTION

This then is the message which we have heard of Him, and declare unto you, that God is light, and in Him is no darkness at all. If we say that we have fellowship with Him, and walk in darkness, we lie, and do not the truth: But if we walk in the light, as He is in the light, we have fellowship one with another, and the blood of Jesus Christ His Son cleanseth us from all sin (1 John 1:5-7).

The believer's fellowship in Christ is one of the greatest experiences in life. Not only is it fellowship with those of "like precious faith," but most importantly "with the Father, and with His Son Jesus Christ." When one enters into this fellowship, he discovers "joy unspeakable and full of glory" (1 Peter 1:8).

The Apostle John gives a description of the message he and his fellow workers had been declaring: "This then is the message which we have heard of Him, and declare unto you, that God is light, and in Him is no darkness at all." Obviously it is the antinomian heresy that is in mind here. The teaching that one could be a Christian while continuing to live in sin had become quite popular. The truth of God was being disregarded, which resulted in widespread disobedience among professed believers. This teaching also identified evil with God and created serious problems in the church.

John sought to combat their error by describing God's true nature: "God is light, and in Him is no darkness at all." Throughout the Scriptures, light is used as a symbol of purity and holiness while darkness represents sin and wickedness. It is not possible for the Lord Jehovah to be associated with sin, for "God is light." This means that He is holy in every respect of His being.

Throughout the Old Testament, the prophets proclaimed the Lord as the "Holy One." Isaiah used this description some thirty times. The Psalmist said, with rapturous praise, "Exalt the LORD our God, and worship at His holy hill; for the LORD our God is holy" (Psalm 99:9). It is impossible for God to participate in any way with evil, for such would oppose His nature. "Thou art of purer eyes than to behold evil, and canst not look on iniquity" (Habakkuk 1:13).

Being righteous, God created a holy universe. Later, He created a man and woman who were also holy. Adam and Eve and all of nature prospered in the holiness of God. This happy state was interrupted by a catastrophe. Endowed with free will, Adam and Eve were tempted and chose to disobey God. The sorrowful result was that "sin entered into the world, and death by sin; and so death passed upon all men, for that all have sinned" (Romans 5:12).

God did not create Adam and Eve to be puppets. Providing them with freedom of choice, He created them holy. But not satisfied with God's best, Adam and Eve chose evil, and all of civilization has suffered ever since.

The choice our first parents made did not thwart God's intention for man's holiness. He sent His holy and sinless Son into the world to die for unholy and sinful mankind. Those who believe on the Son are forgiven of their sins and become the recipients of God's righteousness. "For [God] hath made [Christ] to be sin for us, who knew no sin; that we might be made the righteousness of God in Him" (2 Corinthians 5:21).

Because of the failure of the first man, unredeemed men have "loved darkness rather than light" (John 3:19). But God's concern is that they come to the light. To bridge the gap between light and darkness, there had to be One who was perfect in His deity as well as sinless in His humanity. Only such a One could approach the Father in Heaven and humans on the earth. Jesus Christ, the Son of God, was that One. "For there is one God, and one mediator between God and men, the man Christ Jesus; Who gave Himself a ransom for all, to be testified in due time" (1 Timothy 2:5).

Because of the divine provision of Jesus Christ as the Sin-bearer, any human may experience the holiness of God. If he sincerely repents and receives Jesus Christ into his life, he will become a "new man, which after God is created in righteousness and true holiness" (Ephesians 4:24). It must be understood, however, that it is impossible for anyone to be a "new man" apart from receiving Jesus Christ into his life.

Millions in the world are attempting to produce holiness in the energy of the flesh. Ignoring the claims of Christ, they live carelessly day after day, disregarding the truth of Scripture, trying to provide their own way of salvation. But God's Word declares that salvation is "not by works of righteousness which we have done, but according to [God's] mercy" (Titus 3:5). What man does can never blot out his sin. The best person in the world is condemned to hell until he receives Christ, for his dead works can never produce holiness.

It is said that the architect and builder of Saint Paul's Cathedral in London ran short of funds during the construction. Huge columns were needed to support the roof. In an attempt to avert a financial loss, he made them hollow and filled them with rubbish.

During the ensuing years, the many thousands of visitors and worshipers were unaware that the great pillars were not solid. No one was told. In time, however, the roof began to sag, and it was obvious that something was wrong. An extensive investigation revealed the reason: the columns were not strong enough to bear the weight of the massive roof.

Many a life, which outwardly appears to be pleasing in the eyes of men because of good motives and worthy ambitions, falls far short of God's standard, which is perfection. Since no human is perfect, his only hope is to trust in the Holy One, Jesus Christ, the Son of God. "God is light, and in Him is no darkness at all." In Christ, victory over sin is won and the holiness of God is experienced.

If one has received Christ into his life, he will evidence this by faithful obedience. If, on the other hand, he claims to be a follower of Christ while continuing in the old paths of sin, it is clear that his profession is unreal. "If we say that we have fellowship with Him, and walk in darkness, we lie, and do not the truth."

Those who have entered into a personal relationship with the Father through the Son should reveal the holiness of God. "Ye shall be holy; for I am holy" (Leviticus 11:44). "I am the light of the world: he that followeth Me shall not walk in darkness, but shall have the light of life" (John 8:12). It is the normal experience for the believer to show forth the holiness of God.

If one professes Christ and does not live for the Lord, all his talk and activity for God are meaningless. Paul wrote, "As ye have therefore received Christ Jesus the Lord, so walk ye in Him" (Colossians 2:6). "Christ died for our sins" (1 Corinthians 15:3), not merely to make an atonement for them, but to deliver us from them. God's people are saved from the darkness of sin to walk in the light. "For Thou hast delivered my soul from death: wilt not Thou deliver my feet from falling, that I may walk before God in the light of the living?" (Psalm 56:13)

It would be well for all who are in Christ to consider, "Is the life I am now living worth the price Christ paid for it?" It is not always easy to live victoriously, but anyone who has been delivered from darkness knows that the Christ-controlled life is the only satisfying life to live.

Jim Vaus discovered this truth a number of years ago. A big job was coming up for him. By tapping wires and delaying teletype messages, Jim and the syndicate could make thousands of dollars at the Saint Louis racetrack. With his electronic devices, their win was sure. Vaus would get a big share of the money won.

Midway in his probable success, Jim quit the job. The crime ring was stunned. No man with the inside knowledge of crime Vaus had was allowed to quit and live.

It wasn't long until Jim's boss phoned. "Remember this: No one quits on Andy, see?" Andy threatened to kill Vaus as he had killed others.

Jim could face this threat with confidence and peace because, a few nights before, his life had been changed by turning it over to Christ. Now he was called upon to face the first big test of the Lord's sufficiency.

A few days after the phone call, Jim happened to look out the window. A big black car turned into his driveway and several men got out. Andy was in the lead. As they spread out to block any attempt to escape, Vaus went out to meet them. Immediately he began telling them of his decision to follow Christ. After speaking at length, he invited Andy and his men to leave their life of sin. Unwilling, they climbed back into the car and drove away.

Jim Vaus had some difficult days following his conversion. Not only did the syndicate leaders threaten to kill him, but in repaying his debts, caused by crime, he went bankrupt. Without money or a job, he lost his beautiful home. But the Lord never failed His servant. Jim has been used in a mighty way to touch untold numbers of lives for Christ and to see them walk in the holiness of God.

How important that we ask ourselves frequently, "Am I real, or am I only pretending?" Do we really know Christ? "If we say that we have fellowship with Him, and walk in darkness, we lie, and do not the truth." Truth must not only be spoken, but lived. The situation becomes extremely distressing as we see the way some of our church people live. In the singing of hymns they confess their submission to Christ, but in their living they deny Him by what they say and do. To hear some of them talk, you would think they are really yielded to Christ's control; but to watch them, you wonder.

What if one of the players on a basketball team did everything he could to help the opposing team? He would not be left in the game very long. The coach would have him on the bench in a matter of minutes. Yet, think of those in the game of life, who profess to be followers of Christ while helping Satan and his cause by their inconsistent living. They claim to "have fellowship with God," but "walk in darkness." John says they are lying. Of course, they are not deceiving God; they are deceiving themselves.

Judas was such an example. Doubtless, he talked in the same manner as the other disciples in his appreciation for Jesus. But Judas was different. It is noticeable that whenever he addressed the Saviour directly he never called Jesus Lord. This is certainly in keeping with 1 Corinthians 12:3 where Paul tells us "that no man can say that Jesus is the Lord, but by the Holy Ghost." It is evident that Judas had never really come to know the Lord.

Even though Judas was able to deceive the other disciples into thinking that he was one of them, Christ knew differently. Our Lord said, "Woe unto that man by whom the Son of man is betrayed! It had been good for that man if he had not been born" (Matthew 26:24). On another occasion, He said, "Have not I chosen you twelve, and one of you is a devil?" (John 6:70) At the last supper, as our Lord told of His forthcoming crucifixion, Satan entered into Judas (John 13:27). It is impossible for Satan to enter the life of one born of the Holy Spirit. In His high priestly prayer, our Lord stated, "Those that Thou gavest Me I have kept, and none of them is lost, but the son of perdition" (John 17:12). The climax to Judas's wasted, hypocritical life came by suicide. What a tragedy, to live each day posing as a follower of God.

Have you ever wondered why Jesus chose Judas to be one of His disciples? Did He not know what Judas would do and what he would be like? Of course He did. He knew all about Judas. Why then did He allow him to pretend to be a true disciple? He did it for the same reason that He allows people to pretend in our day: He loves them and is concerned about them. He is desirous that they will forsake their hypocrisy and enter into the reality of a heart-belief. In mercy, He gives them every opportunity possible to repent of their sin and believe. In the example of Judas, God has allowed us to see how close one might be to the truth and yet miss it altogether. Let none of us fall into the same error.

As the believer lives in obedience to God, he enjoys the blessing of God. Disobedience always produces disharmony. Sin disrupts, while righteousness results in peace and happiness. "But if we walk in the light, as He is in the light, we have fellowship one with another."

Though it is true that when believers are right with the Lord, they enjoy happy fellowship together, in 1 John 1:7 John has in mind the ultimate fellowship he had written about in verse 3: "Truly our fellowship is with the Father, and with His Son Jesus Christ."

This blessed fellowship with the Lord will enable the child of God to experience God's peace in spite of hardships and trials. Paul suffered much in his quest to make Christ known, but he could say, "Therefore I take pleasure in infirmities, in reproaches, in necessities, in persecutions, in distresses for Christ's sake: for when I am weak, then am I strong" (2 Corinthians 12:10). His trials made him weak, but his fellowship with God made him strong, enabling him to face the severest conflicts.

How does the believer sustain his fellowship with the Lord? John says, "Walk in the light, as He is in the light." We are to obey God and do His will. We must seek to follow His leading in everything. We cannot afford to choose our own paths and follow our own ways; such never provides happiness. Daily we must pray, "Teach me Thy way, O LORD" (Psalm 27:11). God's way is always best, for it is the way of holiness, the way of "light."

It is easy to distinguish the devil's way from God's, for sin is always part of the devil's way. Never is this the case when "we walk in the light, as He is in the light." God's way is without lying, cheating, immorality, unkindness, or sin of any kind. This is the way of blessing.

The real motive to "walk in the light, as [God] is in the light," is that we might have fellowship with God. Some have thought erroneously that the reason Christians no longer do the things they used to do is because of the fear of being punished by God. Not only does one receive victory to refrain from former sins following conversion, even more, he has a desire to please the Lord. This is born out of love, not fear.

While refusing to do wrong, a little boy was taunted by his friend, "You are afraid that your dad will hurt you." "Not really," said the boy. "I am afraid that I will hurt him."

Born-again believers are in fellowship with God Almighty. Because of this, they are not fearful of being punished by God; their punishment was absorbed by Christ at the cross. They "walk in the light" that they might please the Lord and do His will. True believers know the joy of obedience.

If the child of God yields to temptation, God has made a provision: "The blood of Jesus Christ His Son cleanseth us from all sin." The blood is always efficacious. It is without meaning to the hypocrite, but to the one who is sincere before God, there is continual forgiveness at any time and at any place. Christ's blood keeps on cleansing from sin. It never stops.

Christ's blood is sufficient for "all sin," whether it be the sin of the repentant soul turning to Jesus for salvation, or the sin which is the result of daily defilement in the life of the believer.

God promises, "The blood of Jesus Christ His Son cleanseth us from all sin." Would you have fellowship with the eternal God? Then, "walk in the light, as He is in the light," allowing Him to keep you clean through the blood, as you confess all sin to Him. Let Him live through you as you seek by His grace daily to obey and please Him in everything.

DECEPTION

If we say that we have no sin, we deceive ourselves, and the truth is not in us. If we confess our sins, He is faithful and just to forgive us our sins, and to cleanse us from all unrighteousness. If we say that we have not sinned, we make Him a liar, and His word is not in us (1 John 1:8-10).

Evidence of new life in Christ is discernible when one is walking in the light, as Christ is in the light. For one to say that he belongs to God, while living in sin, is to prove himself a liar. Since "God is light, and in Him is no darkness at all," those who follow Him will reveal His light. As long as the believer reveals the light of Christ, he enjoys fellowship with God. Should he sin, cleansing is available immediately on the basis of Christ's blood that was shed at Calvary.

There is possible deception: "If we say that we have no sin, we deceive ourselves, and the truth is not in us." This appears to be an attack on an error advanced by the deluded Gnostics who taught that, though matter was sinful, the soul was without sin. Such teaching was a denial of what the Lord Jesus taught: "For from within, out of the heart of men, proceed evil thoughts, adulteries, fornications, murders, thefts, covetousness, wickedness, deceit, lasciviousness, an evil eye, blasphemy, pride, foolishness: All these evil things come from within, and defile the man" (Mark 7:21-23). The various forms of wickedness listed here are the fruits of man's sinful nature. If anyone says that he has no sin, he deceives himself.

This error was existent not only in John's day; it has continued to the present. There are those who teach that a Christian can reach a state of sanctification whereby the Adamic nature is eradicated completely, allowing him to live in a state of sinless perfection. Anyone who believes this is deceiving himself, but only himself; those who observe him know that he is not perfect. Even if one appeared to be sinless, there would still be a problem: "The LORD seeth not as man seeth; for man looketh on the outward appearance, but the LORD looketh on the heart" (1 Samuel 16:7).

The Bible makes it clear that the old nature continues, even after conversion. Though one's sins are forgiven, the sinful Adamic nature must be kept constantly under Christ's control. Let no one think he can jump the hurdle of sin once for all. Paul was aware of this. Even though he was a mature saint, he confessed, "I find then a law, that, when I would do good, evil is present with me. For I delight in the law of God after the inward man. But I see another law in my members, warring against the law of my mind, and bringing me into captivity to the law of sin which is in my members. O wretched man that I am! who shall deliver me from the body of this death?" (Romans 7:21-24) Who of us has not, at some time, sensed this same defeat in the conflict of the old and new natures? The apostle knew who could give him victory over his sinful nature: "I thank God through Jesus Christ our Lord" (Romans 7:25). Though the pull of sin was strong at all times, Paul realized that, as he relied completely on Christ, he could enjoy lasting victory over sin.

A middle-aged pastor had an affair. His wife became aware of the infatuation and saw it grow into something serious and destructive. Later, the church board became aware of it, and asked the pastor to resign. Realizing his error, the pastor broke the relationship with the other woman and returned to his wife, but because of what had transpired, it became necessary for the pastor to give up the ministry and go into business.

Some weeks later, however, he began to visit other churches, hoping that the past might be forgotten. One Sunday, he and his wife entered a new church at Sunday school time. They were met at the door by a pleasant gentleman, who told of several classes for adults and their corners of study. Then he asked, "Which one would you like?"

The former pastor replied with remorse, "I guess I belong in the nursery department."

This answer was not understood by the gentleman, but it certainly could not have been more honest. The former pastor was to be respected for recognizing this and admitting it. He had learned at first hand that "The heart is deceitful above all things, and desperately wicked: who can know it?" (Jeremiah 17:9)

As it pertains to personal sin, any believer who will be honest with himself will admit freely that he, too, belongs in the nursery department. This is why we must depend on Christ constantly. He is the only perfect One. It is He who gives Himself to us to enable us to overcome the temptations to our sinful natures. David declared, "Our help is in the name of the LORD, who made heaven and earth" (Psalm 124:8).

When Daniel W. Whittle read the words of the hymn entitled, "I Need Thee Every Hour," he said, "That is not enough for me. I need Him every moment." Immediately, he sat down and wrote the words of the inspiring hymn:

> Moment by moment I'm kept in His love;
> Moment by moment I've life from above;
> Looking to Jesus till glory doth shine;
> Moment by moment, O Lord, I am Thine.

Victorious and fruitful living is a moment-by-moment experience. As we depend on Christ entirely, He provides the strength and power we need. Our only victory over sin is in Him, never in ourselves.

In contrast to those who say they have no sin, sincere believers can maintain a happy and right relationship to God on the basis of confession.

At the moment of conversion, God forgives all sin: past, present, and future. But something further must be done about daily defilement. All of us are plagued by evil thoughts and actions: "If we confess our sins, He is faithful and just to forgive us our sins, and to cleanse us from all unrighteousness." Here is a tremendous promise.

When a believer has done the wrong thing, does he lose his salvation? Not at all. He has, however, broken fellowship with God. As a result, he is out of harmony with the Lord. But he need not remain in this state for he can "confess" to the Lord and be restored to fellowship immediately.

To "confess" to the Lord is to tell Him we are sorry

for the specific sin we have committed. Of course, He knows what we have done. It is the motive of the believer's heart that is important in confession. Psalm 51 evidences David's sorrow and sincerity as he confesses to the Lord, following his sin with Bathsheba. David's submissive attitude is seen throughout the Psalm.

If others are involved in our sin, in order for our confession to be acceptable to God, we must ask forgiveness of those whom we have offended. We should not wait, but go immediately to anyone involved and make matters right. Irrespective of who is to blame, to expect God's forgiveness, we must seek our neighbor's forgiveness. The Lord Jesus Himself emphasized this: "Therefore if thou bring thy gift to the altar, and there rememberest that thy brother hath ought against thee; Leave there thy gift before the altar, and go thy way; first be reconciled to thy brother, and then come and offer thy gift" (Matthew 5:23-24). This is not easy to do, but the obedient believer will be blessed in doing it. If we are truly repentant in our confession, we are in a position to claim the promise that God "is faithful and just to forgive us our sins, and to cleanse us from all unrighteousness."

There are three words here that must not be overlooked. "He is faithful." Christians have been heard to say that they had confessed to God, but did not "feel" forgiven. God's forgiveness depends solely upon His love and mercy, not our feelings. There is never a time when He is not faithful. "Know therefore that the LORD thy God, He is God, the faithful God, which keepeth covenant and mercy with them that love Him and keep His commandments to a thousand generations" (Deuteronomy 7:9). He is "the faithful God" who never changes. One may not "feel" forgiven because of the guilt associated with disobedience. But God is still "the faithful God."

Thus, never forget, if you are honest and sincere in your confession, God will be faithful in His forgiveness.

Not only is the Lord "faithful" in His forgiveness, He is "just." This has to do with the righteous nature of God. Because of His righteous nature, there is never a time when He can fail His promises. We are assured of forgiveness on the basis of confession because God cannot fail or lie. For this reason, believers need never beg God for forgiveness. Our responsibility is to confess. If we do, God forgives. His forgiveness is promised on the basis of our confession.

"Confess," as it is used in verse 9, is not a once-and-for-all experience. We should confess to the Lord immediately whenever sin is committed. One should never wait until evening or morning prayer time for confession, which could result in periods of sad defeat in the believer's life. Sin must always be confessed immediately to enjoy fellowship with the Lord.

On one occasion, while speaking, D. L. Moody was interrupted by a theological student. This irritated the great preacher, resulting in an unkind response to the student's question. Moody continued to speak, but not for long. There was a pause, and then he said, "Friends, I want to confess before you all that I made a great mistake. I answered my young brother down there foolishly. I am sorry, and I claim God's forgiveness." Before anyone could realize what was happening, Moody left the platform, rushed over to the young man and asked his forgiveness. Someone in the audience, who had heard Moody preach many of his Spirit-filled messages, was heard to comment, "This is the greatest thing I ever saw D. L. Moody do."

As the believer walks with the Lord in fellowship with Him, he becomes extremely sensitive toward sin. Merely rationalizing or trying to explain it away in one's mind is not enough. To enjoy the continued blessing of God on his life, his only recourse is to confess. Nowhere in the Bible are we told of anyone who was ever forgiven any other way than by confessing to the Lord. Confession is the key that unlocks the door to God's blessing. Sin must not be allowed to smolder in the heart! We must get rid of it fast!

David prayed, "Create in me a clean heart, O God; and renew a right spirit within me" (Psalm 51:10). This should be the desire of every believer. God has given us eternal deliverance from sin and all its consequences. Let's not live in daily defilement since God's forgiveness is always available. Our God is not a policeman, waiting to punish us if we fail. He is a sympathetic, loving Heavenly Father who longs to help us, whatever our need. Especially is He desirous of forgiving us of all our sins and cleansing us from all unrighteousness.

"If we say that we have not sinned, we make Him a liar, and His word is not in us." In verse 8, the apostle declared that anyone who said he had no sin, deceived himself. It is bad enough to deceive one's self, but this does not begin to compare with the seriousness of calling God a liar.

In verse 10, the apostle was writing about those who say, "we have not sinned" at any time, either before or after conversion. To make such a statement not only declares God to be a liar, but reveals profound ignorance of the Word of God. From Genesis to Revelation, God has given us scores of examples of men and women who failed because of sin. The Bible does not glorify humanity; it simply reveals it as it is. There is not a perfect character presented in the Bible other than Jesus Christ. God declared "For all have sinned, and come short of the glory of God" (Romans 3:23). Sin has always been, and will continue to be, a distinct mark of human nature. To deny this is to reject the truth of God. Jesus said, "Ye do err, not knowing the scriptures" (Matthew 22:29). To refuse to acknowledge the fact of sin is to claim God to be a liar and His truth to be worthless.

The purpose of Christ's first advent was to provide deliverance from sin. He "came not to call the righteous, but sinners to repentance" (Luke 5:32). Thus a denial of sin is a rejection of the purpose and plan of the cross.

Sin is real, even more real than any of us can understand. It is always a problem. It hinders the believer's effectiveness for God. It robs him of the joy of the Lord. It keeps him from many of the blessings God desires to bestow upon him. It is something with which the believer must contend every hour of every day. For this reason we must keep in a right relationship with Jesus, the Son of God, for He is our strength to overcome sin.

At the root of our sinfulness is our selfish heart, which resists the work of God within us. This was the problem of the children of Israel during their many years of wilderness wanderings. It took forty long years to make an eleven-day journey. Because of their selfish resistance to God's plan, they averaged thirty-three funerals a day for forty years.

Though we may not deny the reality of sin as a fact, by our capricious attitude it is evident that we are denying it experientially. The Apostle Paul dealt with this problem in his life: "But I keep under my body, and bring it into subjection: lest that by any means, when I have preached to others, I myself should be a castaway" (1 Corinthians 9:27). Though he desired to obey the Lord, the self-life was a constant hindrance. Realizing this, Paul did something about it: "I keep under my body." He kept the evil intent of his heart under control. All praise went to the only One who could do it: "Thanks be to God, which giveth us the victory through our Lord Jesus Christ" (1 Corinthians 15:57).

Let us face the reality of our sinful hearts in the same way. Begin with a fresh commitment of your entire life to God. Then ask Him to take complete control. Should you yield to temptation in the future, confess immediately. Then thank Him for forgiveness and live in the blessedness of a Christ-controlled life.

2

DESIGNATION

My little children, these things write I unto you, that ye sin not. And if any man sin, we have an advocate with the Father, Jesus Christ the righteous: and He is the propitiation for our sins: and not for ours only, but also for the sins of the whole world (1 John 2:1-2).

These verses continue the concluding thought of the previous chapter: When the believer sins, he should confess to God and be forgiven immediately.

"Little children" seems to be one of the Apostle John's favorite expressions, which he uses nine times in this Epistle. It was also used by our Lord as He spoke with His disciples. Possibly it was then that John first learned to appreciate these words.

"Little children" refers to those born into the family of God when they trusted Christ as Saviour and Lord. Some of them were being deceived by false teachers. John appealed to them as "little children" to be extremely careful what they believed. He wrote as one mature in the faith, who had "heard" and "seen" the Lord. He didn't want them to get the wrong impression and think that because they had a sinful nature it was necessary to continue in sin. Believers have a mighty Lord who can give victory over any sin.

This, of course, is not true in the life of the unsaved. The only strength unbelievers have to overcome sin is the strength of the flesh. Since the flesh is sinful, it is impossible to fight sin with sin. Nowhere in the Bible does God tell unbelievers to "sin not." But He does tell His "little children," those who have experienced new life in Christ, to stop sinning. "My little children, these things write I unto you, that ye sin not."

The believer can overcome any sin, if he trusts Christ for the power. Paul expressed this important truth well: "But thanks be to God, which giveth us the victory through our Lord Jesus Christ" (1 Corinthians 15:57). According to this, God gives believers victory. Since there can be no defeat in victory, even though he has a sinful nature the believer can overcome any or all sin in the power of Christ.

Leslie Weatherhead tells of reading a book, some years ago, entitled *The Road Mender*, by Michael Fairless. Mr. Weatherhead says, "For years I thought the author of the book must be a wonderful naturalist with a style of poetic prose that helped one to revel in the glories of nature. Later, however, it was learned the 'Michael Fairless' was the pen name of a sick woman who was dying. Her body was bound by disease, but her mind was gloriously free."

Though the believer lives in a body of sinful flesh, he need not be dominated by the flesh, for in Christ he is free. "For the law of the Spirit of life in Christ Jesus hath made me free from the law of sin and death" (Romans 8:2).

But does it really work? Considering our own lives and past failures, we may have doubts. Let's face it—there have been times when we failed, but this was not a failure on God's part. We failed to appropriate the power of Christ by not submitting to His control. He refuses to work through us until we let Him work in us. Sin cannot be overcome by a determined effort of the flesh. God's plan demands a yielded life. We must come to the end of ourselves. Realizing our extreme weakness, with full dependence on Christ, we must claim Him as our Victor.

Paul did not instruct young Timothy to "fight the good fight." This would have been nothing more than a struggle culminating in defeat. The admonition was, "Fight the good fight of faith" (1 Timothy 6:12).

We are told to "Resist the devil" (James 4:7). This is a serious responsibility. If left to ourselves, it would be utterly impossible. But before Paul wrote this, he said, "Submit yourselves therefore to God." This is the secret in resisting the devil.

The same thought is expressed in 1 Peter 5:8: "Be sober, be vigilant; because your adversary the devil, as a roaring lion, walketh about, seeking whom he may devour." In the next verse, we are told how this can be done: "Whom resist stedfast in the faith." There must be unreserved dependence on the Lord: "in the faith."

Even the angels would not presume to stand against Satan without God's strength. "Michael the archangel, when contending with the devil he disputed about the body of Moses, durst not bring against him a railing accusation, but said, The Lord rebuke thee" (Jude 9). If the angelic beings find it necessary to depend upon the Lord in their conflict with Satan and sin, can we do any less?

Thus, for the believer in Christ, there is no such thing as a hopeless case, as far as sin's power is concerned. As we yield to Christ's control, we enjoy His victory.

Following conversion, the believer is commanded not to sin. But if he does, then what? Does he lose his salvation? Must he get saved all over again? Definitely not! One cannot lose his salvation if he was genuinely saved in the first place. Of course, if his was only a mental or emotional experience, he could fall away. But if he was sincere in receiving Jesus Christ into his life, he was saved for eternity.

This certainly is verified by our Lord Himself: "My sheep hear My voice, and I know them, and they follow Me. And I give unto them eternal life; and they shall never perish, neither shall any man pluck them out of My hand. My Father, which gave them Me, is greater than all; and no man is able to pluck them out of My Father's hand" (John 10:28-29). What did Jesus say we receive the moment we believe on Him? "Eternal life!" There is nothing in these verses to suggest that if the believer sins, he is lost. It is just the opposite: "They shall never perish."

What actually happens is, when the believer sins, though he does not lose his salvation, he severs his fellowship with God. As the result, his prayer life is hindered and his usefulness for God is curtailed until he confesses to the Lord and receives forgiveness.

John's phrase, as used here, "If any man sin," does not refer to the habitual, willful practice of sin. If one professes to be a believer in Christ and continues to live in sin, it is obvious that he has never really entered the family of God. Paul refers to this in Romans 6:1-2: "What shall we say then? Shall we continue in sin, that grace may abound? God forbid. How shall we, that are dead to sin, live any longer therein?"

What John is writing about is a single act of sin. He pleads with the believer in Christ not to sin; but if he does, his advocate, Jesus Christ, is ready immediately to plead his case before the Father.

Christ is in a position to do this because He is "Jesus

Christ *the righteous.*" Not only is He without sin, but He died and shed His blood for our sins. On this basis, forgiveness and restoration are available for the repentant believer immediately upon confession of his sin.

Doubtless you have had the experience of feeling unworthy of God's forgiveness after yielding to temptation. In no sense of the word is forgiveness ever based upon our worthiness. It is our Advocate who is worthy. "Jesus Christ the righteous" has come to our side to help, as well as present our case to the Father, thus making forgiveness a reality.

Frequently, after we confess to the Lord, Satan plagues us with false accusations in an attempt to make us feel as if we are not fully forgiven. Don't listen to him! God has declared that we are forgiven. As the result, we are back in fellowship with Him. For this reason, we should forget the past and continue to walk by faith. Learn from the experience. Let it be a reminder of the weakness of the flesh so that you will depend more completely on Christ.

Believers can be thankful that God has made such a marvelous provision for forgiveness. This should not, however, cause us to become careless in our relationship to sin. We who love Christ must pray for a holy hatred of sin. Realizing that all the suffering and misery in the world is the result of sin, it should cause us to heed John's words and "sin not."

My first pastorate was in a small church in central Illinois. Living in our neighborhood was a beautiful, eleven-year-old girl by the name of Shirley Ann Sprenkle. Because Shirley Ann's father was an alcoholic, hers was a very unhappy home.

One Sunday afternoon, Shirley Ann was playing in the living room when her father came home drunk. He was abusive and profane as he argued with his wife. Becoming extremely angry, he dashed to a closet, and grabbed a shotgun. Pointing it at his wife, he threatened to kill her. Accidentally, the gun fired. While trying to help her mother, little Shirley was struck and one side was practically blown away. She was rushed to the hospital, and her father was taken to jail.

The next day the father was granted the privilege of visiting his dying daughter. When Shirley saw him, she smiled and said, "Daddy, please give me a drink."

"The nurse will bring you a drink, Honey," he replied.

After visiting a few more minutes, he could stand it no longer, and started to leave. He almost collapsed as Shirley cried and pleaded, "Daddy, please wait till I get my drink." Shirley Ann died not long after her father left.

I have thought of Shirley Ann Sprenkle many times down through the years. That sorrowful experience continues to warn me of the power of sin and its consequences. Satan has respect for no one. This is why it is so important that we, who know Christ, follow Him closely and "walk in the light, as He is in the light." As we do, "the blood of Jesus Christ" will keep cleansing us from sin so we can live in the victory of Christ.

Are you experiencing His victory in your life? Maybe you say, "Not exactly. I seem to have real problems along this line. I believe in Christ, but I keep yielding to temptation." Are you spending the time you should in God's Word each day, feeding on the truth that can sustain you when tempted? Have you learned the value of communing with God in prayer? Are you permitting Christ to be your Lord in everything? Or, are you trying to live in your own strength? If you are, it is understandable why you are failing. Trust your Advocate; He cannot fail. He will help you at any time you allow Him. "Our help is in the name of the LORD, who made heaven and earth" (Psalm 124:8).

The huge jets that fly the skies are built to cross the oceans and reach their destinations. But occasionally something goes wrong. This is why inflatable rafts are kept in the planes; a provision has been made.

Believers are called not to sin. But in the event that they do, God has made a provision. Forgiveness is available on the basis of confession, made possible through Jesus Christ, our Advocate.

Not only is Christ our advocate, "He is the propitiation for our sins." More than this, He is the propitiation "also for the sins of the whole world." The blood that was shed at Calvary provided atonement for all who believe on Jesus Christ. The sacrifice of Christ is sufficient for all of us who have trusted in the Lord. At the same time, it is also sufficient for all who have not yet believed, if they come to Him.

The word "propitiation" has to do with satisfaction. The righteous demands of the law were satisfied by the sacrifice of the all-righteous Son of God on the cross. Believers can rejoice because forgiveness for sin is always available since Christ "is the propitiation for our sins." But since Christ is the propitiation "for the sins of the whole world," we are obligated to all in the world who are outside of Christ to get God's message of forgiveness to them. We cannot rest or content ourselves until this task is completed. Paul said, "I am debtor both to the Greeks, and to the Barbarians; both to the wise, and to the unwise" (Romans 1:14). We are not debtors to God, for the price of our sins has been paid completely. We are, however, debtors to those who do not know that Christ is their propitiation for sin. We owe every unsaved person an opportunity to hear the gospel at least once.

Among other things, God saved us to be His witnesses. Our Lord said, "Ye have not chosen Me, but I have chosen you, and ordained you, that ye should go and bring forth fruit (John 15:16). Helping the lost to find Christ is not the only way to bear fruit, but it is one way. God has called every believer to this responsibility. "Ye shall be witnesses unto Me both in Jerusalem, and in all Judea, and in Samaria, and unto the uttermost part of the earth" (Acts 1:8). Here we are told of the world-wide coverage for which Christ is the propitiation. He is concerned about everyone in all the world. If we are His followers, we should have this same concern.

We need to remind ourselves constantly that there is only one propitiation for sin. Some people appear to have the mistaken notion that if a person is religious, that is all that is necessary. The Bible makes it clear that Christ is the only way into Heaven. The words of Acts 4:12 cannot be misunderstood, "Neither is there salvation in any other: for there is none other name under heaven given among men, whereby we must be saved."

Silver Bridge was a 1700-foot suspension bridge over the Ohio River, connecting West Virginia and Ohio. For forty years this beautiful bridge served the community well. But on December 15, 1967, the bridge collapsed without warning. Approximately seventy-five cars and trucks were on the bridge at the time. All were plunged headlong into the river below. Many persons lost their lives.

Silver Bridge was a splendid specimen of man's work and served its purpose well for a time. But because man is not perfect, his works are not perfect. They stand in constant need of watching, strengthening, and even replacing.

How different is the bridge into Heaven. It will never collapse. It cannot fail. For Christ is infinitely perfect. "He is the propitiation for our sins: and not for ours only, but for the sins of the whole world." Anyone who places faith in the Son of God for salvation will never be disappointed; he will reach his destination safely.

Have you trusted Christ for your salvation? If not, He is ready to receive you, if only you will trust Him.

DEMONSTRATION

And hereby we do know that we know Him, if we keep His commandments. He that saith, I know Him, and keepeth not His commandments, is a liar, and the truth is not in him. But whoso keepeth His word, in him verily is the love of God perfected: hereby know we that we are in Him. He that saith he abideth in Him ought himself also so to walk, even as He walked. Brethren, I write no new commandment unto you, but an old commandment which ye had from the beginning. The old commandment is the word which ye have heard from the beginning. Again, a new commandment I write unto you, which thing is true in Him and in you: because the darkness is past, and the true light now shineth. He that saith he is in the light, and hateth his brother, is in darkness even until now. He that loveth his brother abideth in the light, and there is none occasion of stumbling in him. But he that hateth his brother is in darkness, and walketh in darkness, and knoweth not whither he goeth, because that darkness hath blinded his eyes (1 John 2:3-11).

After one believes on Christ, things should be different as far as his involvement with sin is concerned. Having received a new life, he should abstain from evil with a desire to please the Lord. Several proofs are given whereby one who professes Christ may substantiate his relationship to Christ. If one has truly believed on the Lord, this fact will be demonstrated outwardly.

The true Christian will obey the truth of God: "And hereby we do know that we know Him, if we keep His commandments." The "commandments" do not refer to the Old Testament law only, but to all the precepts of God as given in the Scriptures by the Holy Spirit. Failure to obey these teachings is to negate one's profession of faith: for "He that saith, I know Him, and keepeth not His commandments, is a liar, and the truth is not in him." It is obvious that such a person has never had a heart-experience with Christ, regardless of what he might say. A verbal claim of believing on Christ is not enough. Visible evidence must be given by obedience to the truth.

Notice the work of God's love in the believer's life: "But whoso keepeth His word, in him verily is the love of God perfected: hereby know we that we are in Him." Salvation is made possible through God's love: "We love Him, because He first loved us" (1 John 4:19). God's love does not end after one believes on Christ. It is at work in the believer's life every step of the way. For what purpose? To enable us to obey the Word of God. Our obedience to the Word is an evidence of this fact: "Whoso keepeth His word, in him verily is the love of God perfected."

The word "perfected" has to do with bringing to fruition. The intended purpose of God's love is being fulfilled as the believer obeys God's Word and does His will.

Peter expresses a similar truth: "For the eyes of the Lord are over the righteous, and His ears are open unto their prayers: but the face of the Lord is against them that do evil" (1 Peter 3:12). The contrast is seen between the obedient and the disobedient. Those who obey God experience His love in His watchful care and provision through prayer. The disobedient, on the other hand, have not yet experienced the love of God.

"To obey is better than sacrifice," we are told (1 Samuel 15:22). God will not accept anything in lieu of obedience. Thus the question must be asked frequently, am I obeying God in every area of my Christian experience? Knowing what we should do is not enough: we must do it. Our Lord said, "If ye know these things, happy are ye if ye do them" (John 13:17). Happiness is discovered only as we obey the Lord. It can be known in no other way. Knowledge of spiritual truth is not sufficient; it must be applied.

A study was released by the University of Southern California indicating that one-third of the medical patients in this country ignore what doctors tell them to do. Before the study was completed, the doctors didn't think the figures would be quite that bad. Forty-two per cent estimated that almost all their patients were obeying orders, and forty-seven per cent thought that at least three-fourths were doing what they were told. The survey proved all of them wrong. Only fourteen per cent of the patients always obeyed the physicians and about forty-nine per cent did so "most of the time." Another twenty-three per cent obeyed less than half the time. Nine per cent obeyed "very seldom," and five per cent, "not at all." Strange to say, persons with more severe illnesses were less likely to carry out orders.

The situation is not much different when it comes to the believer doing what God tells him to do. Believers listen to the Word of God preached and taught, but many fail to do it. Indeed, the words of Hebrews 4:2 are most applicable: "But the word preached did not profit them, not being mixed with faith in them that heard it." What a mistake it is to hear God's Word, or to read it, and yet refuse to obey.

A little girl misquoted the words of a familiar hymn: "If there's no other way to be happy in Jesus, then trust and obey." If we fail to respond to the truth, it is evident that many of us would have to agree with those lines.

We should obey the Lord for three reasons: first, whatever our Lord commands us, He really means us to do; secondly, whatever He commands us is always for our good; and thirdly, whatever He commands us, He is able and willing to enable us to do. Thus, let us obey the Lord in everything, that the love of God may be perfected in us, for then we shall know "that we are in Him."

Not only should the believer obey God, he should reveal Him in his life. "He that saith he abideth in Him ought himself also so to walk, even as He walked." Abiding in Christ has to do with more than our position in Him. It is true that anyone who abides in Christ has been born again by the Holy Spirit and has passed from death unto life. But it also has to do with one's present relationship with his Saviour. Is he walking in harmony with his Lord, or does his manner of life betray his profession? The word "ought" comes from a word meaning "to owe to another," referring to a debt that must be paid. Believers are in debt to God to walk in a manner that is well-pleasing in His sight.

How can Christians walk like Christ? The Bible tells us that He "knew no sin" (2 Corinthians 5:21); He "did no sin" (1 Peter 2:22); and "in Him is no sin" (1 John 3:5). Can we live like Christ without sin? Of course not. "To walk, even as He walked," does not infer perfection.

It means that we should pattern our lives after Him.

What are some of the characteristics evidenced in Christ's life? He prayed for His enemies. Even though His persecutors climaxed their atrocities by nailing Him to a cross, He prayed, "Father, forgive them; for they know not what they do" (Luke 23:34).

Christ always pleased the Father. Never did He act in opposition to the divine will. His concern was "not My will, but Thine, be done" (Luke 22:42).

Christ always showed love and kindness, regardless of what had been said or done against Him. It was He who said, "Love your enemies, bless them that curse you, do good to them that hate you, and pray for them which despitefully use you, and persecute you" (Matthew 5:44).

These and many other characteristics of our Lord should be visible in the believer's life. If they are not, we might wonder if the conversion experience was real. Jesus declared, "By their fruits ye shall know them" (Matthew 7:20). Are we walking like Christ, or are we bearing the characteristics of the ungodly? How we answer will give unquestionable evidence of our relationship to the Saviour.

There was a pastor who, after leading a person to Christ, would always say, "Now, I don't know whether you are saved or not. You should know. I think you are, but God knows whether you are or not. Now, the thing you need to do is to go out and prove to everyone that you are." This is splendid advice for any convert.

But please consider a word of caution. Let us not think that we can walk in our own strength as Christ walked. In every attempt to please God, we are confronted by two adversaries, the old nature on the inside, and the devil on the outside. Neither of these can be treated lightly. But irrespective of their power, the believer is the possessor of a greater power. The Lord tells us to walk like Christ, but He also gives us the necessary equipment to do this. Christ not only gives us a standard to live by, He gives us the power to live by the standard.

In spite of all the hardships and afflictions Paul faced, he could say with confidence, "I can do all things through Christ which strengtheneth me" (Philippians 4:13). Paul knew full well that he was unable to do "all things," but he also knew that as he relied upon Christ, "all things" were possible.

Likewise, "all things" are possible for us. But there must be complete reliance on the Son of God. He must be the Master of our lives. This demands unconditional surrender to Him. We must realize from the moment of our conversion until we meet Christ face to face that we are no longer our own but His to do what He wants.

Actually, this is what conversion is all about. Some "join church" and wonder why they do not feel any different. Others have a mere emotional experience, which simply stirs their feelings. These may satisfy for a time, but they do not last. Conversion has to do with a complete change: "Old things are passed away; behold, all things are become new" (2 Corinthians 5:17). When one has experienced conversion, he will walk like Christ. Many temptations will befall him, but he will keep his eyes fixed on the Son of God, and walk steadily, faithfully forward.

A blind man was preparing to cross a busy thoroughfare in New York City with his faithful seeing-eye dog at his side. Suddenly, the dog's ears shot up, the hair on his back bristled, and his tail straightened out. There was a big tomcat off to one side, hissing, with back extended. It almost seemed as if the cat were saying, "I defy you to chase me." At the same time, the dog appeared to be answering "I would just love to chase you, but I have a job to do." As the master started to walk, the dog, with only an occasional glance back at the cat, was faithful as ever in watching for the hazards that might bring injury to his master.

We who are in Christ have a job to do also. It will not always be easy to walk like Christ; there will be difficulties all along the way. But we can be faithful for "greater is He that is in you, than he that is in the world" (1 John 4:4).

Let's settle for nothing less than for a walk that glorifies God. There can be no greater evidence to ourselves, as well as to the world, that we belong to Jesus.

When one is a follower of Christ and is saved, everyone around will know it. Not only because of what the new convert says, but by what he does. One thing he will do is to keep God's commandments, the precepts of God which appear in both the Old and New Testaments. Secondly, he will walk as Christ walked. In God's strength, he will live like Christ. These two things will witness to the fact that he has really met the Lord. John offers a third evidence: "Brethren, I write no new commandment unto you, but an old commandment which ye had from the beginning. The old commandment is the word which ye have heard from the beginning" (1 John 2:7).

This is not something new. There were scores of new doctrines being taught which were not scriptural. But the aged apostle makes it clear that, years before, the message of love was one of the basic teachings of Christ when He was on this earth. He had taught, "Thou shalt love the Lord thy God with all thy heart, and with all thy soul, and with all thy mind. This is the first and great commandment. And the second is like unto it, Thou shalt love thy neighbor as thyself " (Matthew 22:37-39). As far as John was concerned, these precepts were still true and necessary. Nothing new was needed on the subject since they were foundational for the Christian experience.

None of God's truth will ever need revising. What we have received through God's revelation will stand forever. The time will never come when it will be necessary to say, "We made a mistake. We apologize for what has been said in God's Word."

Though the precept of love did not change, something new had been discovered through the understanding of the precept. "Again, a new commandment I write unto you, which thing is true in Him and in you: because the darkness is past, and the true light now shineth." The new principle is embodied in the phrase, "which thing is true in Him and in you." Christ was love and taught love. But how was it possible for believers with sinful natures to practice this love? Only one way: it is known as the believer allows the Christ of love to live through him. "In Him and in you." Paul wrote, "Christ in you, the hope of glory" (Colossians 1:27). This is the believer's only possibility of loving God and his neighbor as Christ commanded. As Christ is permitted to control us, "the true light" will shine, and "the darkness" of hatred will be expelled.

John becomes very stern as he says, "He that saith he is in the light, and hateth his brother, is in darkness even until now." It matters not what one says about his conversion experience if he persists in hating someone. It will be certain that he has not entered into Christ's love, for Christ's love in the believer, evidenced by the believer, is a necessary witness to salvation. Hatred, on the other hand, is a dead giveaway that he has never been converted. He "is in darkness even until now."

In contrast, John says, "He that loveth his brother abideth in the light, and there is none occasion of stumbling in him." To abide in the light is not only to be saved, but to live in fellowship with the Lord. When one does this, he will not be a stumbling block. He will not prevent others from coming to Christ, for they shall see Christ in him.

What has already been said in verse 9 is restated with greater emphasis: "But he that hateth his brother is in darkness, and walketh in darkness, and knoweth not whither he goeth, because that darkness hath blinded his eyes." There is no question about it, the person described here has not come to know Christ. Anyone who is "in darkness," and walking "in darkness," has never known the light of Christ. For this reason, the true believer should be extremely sensitive to the evil of hatred and all of its by-products such as anger, malice, and revenge. He will not allow these to remain in his life. Though there may be times when they might appear, he will confess to God immediately, and if others have been offended, he will be quick to apologize.

Many years, ago, Jonathan Goforth came across a statement by Charles G. Finney that it was useless for Christians to expect revival by simply asking for it without bothering to fulfill the laws that govern spiritual blessing. As soon as Goforth read these words he said, "If Finney is right, then I am going to find out what these laws are, and obey them, no matter what it costs." What was the first law he discovered? The very one he was not prepared to obey, his unwillingness to be reconciled to a fellow missionary. But God bound him to that law until he was prepared to obey. When he did, the clouds burst, revival flooded his life, and everyone he touched.

Have you experienced God's love through Christ? If so, is this love being manifested through you? Are you proving your profession by the way you live, through obedience to God and walking in the light, as He is in the light? Oh, make certain that you belong to Christ. If there are any doubts, receive Him now. He is a God of grace and love, who longs to forgive you of all your sin.

DENUNCIATION

I write unto you, little children, because your sins are forgiven you for His name's sake. I write unto you, fathers, because ye have known Him that is from the beginning. I write unto you, young men, because ye have overcome the wicked one. I write unto you, little children, because ye have known the Father. I have written unto you, fathers, because ye have known Him that is from the beginning. I have written unto you, young men, because ye are strong, and the word of God abideth in you, and ye have overcome the wicked one. Love not the world, neither the things that are in the world. If any man love the world, the love of the Father is not in him. For all that is in the world, the lust of the flesh, and the lust of the eyes, and the pride of life, is not of the Father, but is of the world. And the world passeth away, and the lust thereof: but he that doeth the will of God abideth for ever (1 John 2:12-17).

The believer in Christ lives in the midst of a world system that is evil and corrupt. This, however, does not lessen his responsibility to obey God and do good. For it is evident from these verses that though the child of God is *in* a sinful environment, he is not to be *of* it.

Addressed as "little children," the entire family of God is in John's thoughts: "I write unto you, little children, because your sins are forgiven you for His name's sake." "Little" is used as a term of endearment meaning "dear children." It concerns everyone who has entered into a personal relationship with Jesus Christ.

The noteworthy fact about the people of God is that their "sins are forgiven." What could be more consoling than this. How thrilling it is to know that the very moment one believes on Christ, every sin he has ever committed is forgiven. God has said: "I will forgive their iniquity, and I will remember their sin no more" (Jeremiah 31:34). One may not feel forgiven, considering his horrible past, but God's Word confirms that he is.

Doubtless there have been times when you have had doubts about your salvation. Why? Surely you did not doubt the truth of Scripture. No, it was Satan who got you to doubt, as you considered your sinful past. But as we keep looking to our Lord, we live in the confidence that "there is therefore now no condemnation to them which are in Christ Jesus."

Of course, none of us is worthy of God's forgiveness. We rightfully deserve God's worst. But on the basis of "His name's sake," all is well. Jesus Christ paid the entire price. His sacrifice is sufficient. Nothing more need be said or done. "The blood of Jesus Christ His Son cleanseth us from all sin."

There are three groups of believers who comprise the family of God. First, the "fathers," of whom it is said that they "have known Him that is from the beginning." These are mature believers who have grown "in grace, and in the knowledge of our Lord and Saviour Jesus

Christ" (2 Peter 3:18). They are the "spiritual" men and women as opposed to the "carnal" believers. They could be old or young in their Christian experience. It is not necessarily how long one has been saved that is important, but how well he invests those years for Christ. All of us have known those who have been saved twenty, thirty, or more years, and yet they have remained as spiritual babies. On the other hand, we are aware of those who have been saved only a short time, and yet their day-by-day growth in Christ has been remarkable.

Next, the "young men" are described as those who "have overcome the wicked one." It appears that these were mature saints who assumed leadership roles in the body of Christ. They possessed the strength of youth as they resisted the devil faithfully in doing the work of God.

Regrettably, not all believers "endure unto the end" (Mark 13:13). Too often, we have known of spiritual catastrophes as believers in Christ have yielded to sin, and been "overcome" by "the wicked one." But God always has His faithful "young men" who weather the storms and stand true, whatever the cost.

What is it that provides the spiritual stamina for the "young men"? The answer is plain and simple: "the Word of God abideth in you." Few have known lasting victory over sin and worth-while achievement for God without a substantial knowledge of the Word of God. This Book will keep us from sin, but sin will keep us from this Book. David declared, "Thy Word have I hid in mine heart, that I might not sin against Thee" (Psalm 119:11).

No believer can long resist the enemy without spending time studying and memorizing God's Word. Paul exhorted each of us to "put on the whole armour of God, that ye may be able to stand against the wiles of the devil"

(Ephesians 6:11).

There is a young lady living in western North Carolina, who has practically lost her eyesight. Recognizing the extreme importance of daily strengthening herself in the Word of God, she reads the Bible through once a year. It is not without much difficulty and hardship, for only as she holds it close to her eyes, searching it with a large magnifying glass, can she see the words. All who know this young lady covet her spiritual depth.

How regrettable that many believers with normal eyesight overlook the value of systematic, daily reading and study of the Scriptures. Small wonder that they live in defeat and fail in their witness for Christ.

The apostle writes to "little children," of whom he says, "ye have known the Father" (1 John 2:13). These are not the same as those spoken of previously. John is writing now of those who are young in the faith, and those who fail to grow in the Lord. They have entered the family of God but gone no further. They know the ABC's of the gospel and that is about all. Unfortunately, most every church has a number of these people on the rolls. They join with good intentions, but that is about as far as they go. With a burdened heart, the pastor prays that they might become as the "young men," and the "fathers." He longs that the Spirit of the Lord might get a hold on them and bring them to the place of full commitment to the control of Christ.

We cannot doubt that these people are saved, having "known the Father," but they give little evidence of this experience. They assume practically no responsibility in the Lord's work. Nor are they interested in Bible classes or prayer meetings. They don't participate in the visitation program. They fail to experience the joy of giving to God. Though they are on their way to Heaven, they are still mastered by the self-life, having never known the Spirit-controlled life. They have not yet discovered the peace and joy many Christians talk about. In fact, for them, it almost becomes a burden to be a Christian.

Growth in the Christian life is as important as growth in one's physical life. A baby is loved and cherished by its mother and father, but parents are not satisfied to see their baby remain a baby. They anticipate growth and maturity.

God has concern for His children. Infancy is necessary for the newly-born child of God, but it becomes a shame for anyone to continue in this state. Paul wrote to the Thessalonians: "We are bound to thank God always for you, brethren, as it is meet, because that your faith groweth exceedingly" (2 Thessalonians 1:3). How worth while! Do you have a faith that "groweth exceedingly"? Are you getting stronger in the Lord day by day?

There is a fine line between the "little children" and the unregenerate church member. Paul says, "Examine yourselves, whether ye be in the faith; prove your own selves" (2 Corinthians 13:5). Are you in the faith? Are you a member of the family of God? How can one know he is a member of the family of God? He will be confident that his "sins are forgiven . . . for His name's sake." Forgiveness is through that "Name which is above every name" (Philippians 2:9), the name of Jesus Christ. There is no other way to become a child of God but through the Lord Jesus Christ. When He is received into the life, all of sin is forgiven and salvation is certain.

Those who are in the family of God are told to "love not the world, neither the things that are in the world." The "world" spoken of here does not refer to the earth and all of God's creation, but rather the present world-system of evil of which Satan is the instigator. Satan's dominion is in total opposition to the plan and will of God. It began many decades ago when Satan proudly asserted, "I will be like the most High" (Isaiah 14:14). As the result of self-will, Satan lost his high and lofty estate as an angel of God and was cast out from the Lord's presence. He established his own kingdom, and has sought to rule it in complete disobedience and opposition to God. Those who follow him seem to have a similar objective.

Satan is motivated by selfishness, as opposed to God's selflessness. Satan is always selfish, while God never is. Thus we live in a world of two conflicting kingdoms. Born-again believers should resist the devil and his kingdom of sin and wickedness while doing everything possible to glorify the Lord in a life controlled by Christ. "No man can serve two masters: for either he will hate the one, and love the other; or else he will hold to the one, and despise the other" (Matthew 6:24).

Though Satan was defeated in his attempt to overpower God, he never changed in his attitude or desire. He is as anxious today of possessing the authority and power of "the most High" as he was many thousands of years ago. For scores of centuries, he has been the author of confusion, deceiving millions into following him: "the god of this world hath blinded the minds of them which believe not" (2 Corinthians 4:4).

It is imperative that everyone who professes to belong to Christ break with anything in which Satan has a part. We are exhorted to "come out from among them, and be ye separate, saith the Lord, and touch not the unclean thing; and I will receive you, and will be a Father unto you, and ye shall be My sons and daughters, saith the Lord Almighty" (2 Corinthians 6:17-18). How disturbing it is to see those who say they belong to Christ continuing to participate in the things that dishonor His Name. They claim to be the friends of God, but the Bible tells us otherwise: "Know ye not that the friendship of the world is enmity with God? whosoever therefore will be a friend of the world is the enemy of God" (James 4:4).

How can one love God while being His enemy? "If any man love the world, the love of the Father is not in him." The Holy Spirit Himself declares that it is impossible for one to be a repository for God's love while at the same time loving Satan's world.

No one should miss the point: the Bible teaches separation. It is all or nothing, as far as God is concerned. Though the believer is in the world, he should not be of it.

Consider your own life. Do you love the Lord? The world-test will give the answer. If the world has the greater appeal, you have reason to wonder.

There are those who say they love Christ, and yet they see nothing wrong in participating with the devil's crowd. They seem to have greater enjoyment in the pleasures of the world than with believers in Christ. They are supposed to be good stewards for the Lord, and yet they waste money and time on things that are worthless, while doing little by way of serving the Lord. They have little interest in reading and studying the Word of God, but there is plenty of time for newspapers and magazines. Have these people really met Christ? It is questionable; the normal experience for God's people is to "love not the world, neither the things that are in the world."

Paul wrote in Romans 12:2, "And be not conformed to this world: but be ye transformed by the renewing of your mind, that ye may prove what is that good, and acceptable, and perfect, will of God." Believers in Christ are to live as those who have experienced new life in Christ; not as conformists, but rather, transformists. Having been reborn by the Spirit of God, they are to please the Lord, even though they live in a world that is filled with corruption, hatred, and every form of wickedness.

Have you truly met the Saviour? Is He the Lord of your life? If so, day by day, He should become more and more precious to you as the world and its appeals grow less attractive. Should this not be true in your life, claim Christ's victory at this moment through His mighty power. He will enable you to do the things you cannot do. Believe Him; trust Him; and experience great and mighty things in the Lord.

Three characteristics of Satan's world-system are "the lust of the flesh, and the lust of the eyes, and the pride of life" (1 John 2:16).

The "lust of the flesh" has to do with the passionate desires of our evil human nature. Even after one becomes a child of God, the lusts of the flesh are not removed, but they can be controlled. If one professes to follow Christ while responding continually to the desires of his corrupt human nature, he might well wonder if he has really met the Saviour.

The "lust of the eyes," likewise, emanates from the evil nature of man. Without Christ's control, we crave many of the things we see. Being naturally covetous, the selfish heart of man is never satisfied. Regardless of what he has, he always wants more. Our Lord sounded a clear warning, "Take heed, and beware of covetousness: for a man's life consisteth not in the abundance of the things which he possesseth" (Luke 12:15). Enjoyable living is not contingent on things. The worldly man does not realize this. He equates success with the accumulation of things. Thus, what he sees, he wants. Believers need to be watchful of this form of worldliness.

"The pride of life" portrays the vain glory of the man

who depends on his own resources rather than on God's. It is confidence in one's self while neglecting to depend upon Christ and His provision.

None of the three characteristics described here are "of the Father," but "of the world." This "world" will not continue forever, for "The world passeth away, and the lust thereof."

Satan's world-system will come to an abrupt end when the Lord Jesus returns to this earth to establish His kingdom. Paul tells us that "the Lord Jesus shall be revealed from heaven with His mighty angels, in flaming fire taking vengeance on them that know not God, and that obey not the gospel of our Lord Jesus Christ: who shall be punished with everlasting destruction from the presence of the Lord, and from the glory of His power" (2 Thessalonians 1:7-9). At that time, "the lust of the flesh, and the lust of the eyes, and the pride of life" will be done away with forever. Christ will establish His reign of righteousness on the earth. All wickedness will cease, for Satan will be bound for a thousand years, and every knee will bow, and every tongue will confess "that Jesus Christ is Lord, to the glory of God the Father" (Philippians 2:11). From that moment on, never again will believers be plagued by the flesh and its lusts.

During Christ's reign of holiness and purity, everyone will obey Him. There will be no resistance or rebellion until the end of Christ's millennial reign when Satan will be free for a short period. He will deceive a few into thinking they can overthrow Christ. This will be only a feeble attempt for it will be subdued quickly. The great white throne judgment will follow, at which time the wicked dead will be resurrected and judged. They, along with Satan and his emissaries, will be condemned and cast into hell forever.

Since the time for Christ's return appears to be very near, how needful it is that we be absolutely certain that we belong to Him and His kingdom, which "abideth for ever." There will be no end for those who are in Christ for they are possessors of eternal life.

John has given three characteristics of Satan's kingdom, "the lust of the flesh, and the lust of the eyes, and the pride of life." This kingdom, he says, will pass away. In contrast, he lists only one characteristic for God's kingdom, which "abideth for ever": doing "the will of God." Those who are members of this kingdom will give unreserved and devoted obedience to the will and plan of God. God's children should find satisfaction in a life of selfless submission to Christ. The man of the world considers this kind of life ridiculous. But having never experienced new life through Christ, he doesn't know any better.

The child of God has found something wonderful and beautiful. Having been a part of the world and its lusts, he is familiar with its limitations. Having come to Christ, however, he has found peace and blessing never known before. Thus, he considers it a privilege to do "the will of God" with the confidence that he "abideth for ever."

DEFECTION

Little children, it is the last time: and as ye have heard that antichrist shall come, even now are there many anti-christs; whereby we know that it is the last time. They went out from us, but they were not of us; for if they had been of us, they would no doubt have continued with us: but they went out, that they might be made manifest that they were not all of us. But ye have an unction from the Holy One, and ye know all things. I have not written unto you because ye know not the truth, but because ye know it, and that no lie is of the truth. Who is a liar but he that denieth that Jesus is the Christ? He is antichrist, that denieth the Father and the Son. Whosoever denieth the Son, the same hath not the Father: [but] he that acknowledgeth the Son hath the Father also. Let that therefore abide in you, which ye have heard from the beginning. If that which ye have heard from the beginning shall remain in you, ye also shall continue in the Son, and in the Father. And this is the promise that He hath promised us, even eternal life. These things have I written unto you concerning them that seduce you. But the anointing which ye have received of Him abideth in you, and ye need not that any man teach you: but as the same anointing teacheth you of all things, and is truth, and is no lie, and even as it hath taught you, ye shall abide in Him. And now, little children, abide in Him; that, when He shall appear, we may have confidence, and not be ashamed before Him at His coming. If ye know that He is righteous, ye know that every one that doeth righteousness is born of Him (1 John 2:18-29).

Since the present world-system will eventually pass away, the apostle issues a warning to the Lord's people, especially the immature believers: "Little children, it is the last time: and as ye have heard that antichrist shall come, even now are there many antichrists; whereby we know that it is the last time." The "little children" addressed here are the same as those of verse 12. They are either young in the faith or older believers who have not matured. Both of these are an easy mark for Satan and false doctrine.

Since it is the "last time," or more specifically, the "last hour," it is important that Christ's followers be mindful of what is coming. The present church age will be climaxed with the judgment of the seven-year tribulation period, at which time the Antichrist will appear. This is the "man of sin . . . the son of perdition," that Paul spoke about, "Who opposeth and exalteth himself above all that is called God, or that is worshipped; so that he as God sitteth in the temple of God, shewing himself that he is God" (2 Thessalonians 2:3-4). The antichrist will establish a reign of wickedness and bloodshed such as has never been known. It will be short-lived, however, for the King of kings and Lord of lords, Jesus Christ, will return to earth to establish His reign of righteousness.

John reminds us that we are fast approaching the time of the end when the antichrist will appear: one of the signs of his soon appearance is the fact that the spirit of the antichrist will precede him. We cannot deny that this time is here now, for there are many false teachers, deluding the unsaved as well as the saved. The situation is becoming more and more serious every day.

This was also a problem when John wrote. "They went out from us, but they were not of us; for if they had been of us, they would no doubt have continued with us: but they went out, that they might be made manifest that they were not all of us." Some of those he wrote about had been leaders among the believers. They bore all the appearances of being true disciples of Christ, but gradually they embraced the false teachings of their day, and forsook the fellowship of the saints to propagate their erroneous beliefs. It would appear that these defectors had never really experienced the new birth. Having only a mental experience with the Lord, they gave assent with their lips, but denied the truth by their works.

Regrettably, there are many like those described with us today. Many ministers in denominational churches and educators in denominational schools profess to be believers, but in their preaching and teaching they openly deny the cardinal truths of the Christian faith.

Though the works of the false teacher are never commendable, there is a sense in which we respect the honesty of those of John's day. After they embraced false doctrine, they acknowledged their unbelief and left the church. But in our day, there are many religious leaders within the church, who "profess that they know God; but in works they deny Him, being abominable, and disobedient, and unto every good work reprobate" (Titus 1:16). All of this is not without meaning. The increase of apostasy and false teaching in our day is a strong indication that "the coming of the Lord draweth nigh" (James 5:8).

Serious concern has been expressed by some because medical doctors are being deluded into prescribing new and often inadequately tested medicines that have flooded the market. It has been said that one out of every twenty-one hospital beds is occupied by a patient who is there as the result of the prescribed medicines.

It appears that many doctors have been influenced by exaggerated advertising claims from the drug firms.

The seriousness of this problem is easily recognized. To use the wrong medicine would be worse than using no medicine at all. But as serious as this is, it does not in any way compare with the horrible crime on the part of religious leaders, who profess to be teachers of truth and yet consistently provide poison for the soul. This is actually what the false teachers are doing.

If one is a true Christian, having been born of the Spirit, he has no right to listen to, or to support these deceivers in any way. If he does, he is participating in the work of Satan. How can a true child of God support anyone who is against Christ? Those of us who know Him must keep close to Him.

Though the believer should be ever watchful for false teaching, he need not be fearful of it. "Ye have an unction from the Holy One, and ye know all things." The "unction from the Holy One" refers to the believer's anointing with the Spirit, which takes place at the time of his conversion.

When the Old Testament priests were inducted into office, they were anointed with oil. Believers in Christ, the New Testament priests, are anointed with the oil of the Holy Spirit the moment they believe on Christ. At that time, God the Father sends the Holy Spirit to indwell them, never to depart. Our Lord referred to this experience when He declared, "I will pray the Father, and He shall give you another Comforter, that He may abide with you for ever" (John 14:16).

As the result of this anointing, we "know all things." This is not to suggest that we possess unlimited knowledge. There are many things we do not know. What is meant is, that which we know through the teaching of the Holy Spirit concerning the truth, as revealed in the Scriptures, is absolute. Knowledge given through God's Spirit need never be questioned, for what the Spirit gives us through the Scriptures will stand forever. Thus the believer can test any teaching in the light of God's Word and decide through the guidance of the Spirit whether it is truth or error. The Berean saints used this procedure regularly in discerning truth. "They received the word with all readiness of mind, and searched the scriptures daily, whether those things were so" (Acts 17:11). Those saints took nothing for granted. Faithfully, they went to the Scriptures and tested what they heard. Such a practice is extremely worth while.

It was not because the "little children" did not know the truth that John warned them. They had heard the faithful teachers and were knowledgeable. But John was concerned because of the lies that were being propagated. "No lie is of the truth." There is one basic lie that provides unquestionable evidence of a false teacher: "Who is a liar but he that denieth that Jesus is the Christ?"

Because the false teachers did not acknowledge Christ as God's Son, they had no relationship to God, the Father. "He is antichrist, that denieth the Father and the Son. Whosoever denieth the Son, the same hath not the Father: [but] he that acknowledgeth the Son hath the Father also."

It has been said by some that "it doesn't really matter what you believe. After all, eventually we shall all go to the same place." This is a Satanic lie. It does matter what we believe. To believe merely that Jesus Christ is a good man, a great leader, or an inspiring thinker, will save no one. The Bible teaches that He is the virgin-born Son of God, who was crucified for the sins of the world, rose again for our justification, ascended into Heaven, and is coming again. For one to deny these basic truths and to declare himself to be a child of God is a lie.

The Scriptures make it very plain that belief in Jesus Christ as He is presented in the Bible, is God's requisite for salvation. "He that believeth on the Son hath ever-lasting life: and he that believeth not the Son shall not see life; but the wrath of God abideth on him" (John 3:36). There are scores of verses throughout the Bible that present this same fact that salvation is through Jesus Christ, God's Son, and no other way.

There are some who would lead us to believe that as long as one worships God the Father, all is well. But it is impossible to worship God the Father unless one believes on Jesus the Son. "Whosoever denieth the Son, the same hath not the Father: [but] he that acknowledgeth the Son hath the Father also." The Lord Jesus also declared that "no man cometh unto the Father, but by Me" (John 14:6). There is no possible way for anyone to worship the Father other than through the Son.

How can anyone think that God the Father would send His beloved Son into this world of sin to die on a cross, and yet not expect His creatures to honor this sacrifice? This was the greatest event of all history. Jesus Christ came to be the Sin-bearer for all mankind so that all who believe on Him might be eternally saved and go to Heaven. How important it is that everyone give the same respect to Jesus Christ that God the Father gives to Him.

The "little children" are exhorted further to hold fast to the truth so as not to be deceived by the false teachers. Everything should be tested by the atonement of the incarnate Christ. "Let that therefore abide in you, which ye have heard from the beginning." Those who continue in the truth will have no question as to their salvation.

"If that which ye have heard from the beginning shall remain in you, ye also shall continue in the Son, and in the Father."

Though it is not always easy to be a Christian, it is worth it all. Sometimes the way becomes difficult, but it is extremely rewarding: "this is the promise that He hath promised us, even eternal life." Thus, John says, "These things have I written unto you concerning them that seduce you." Be watchful "little children" for Satan's emissaries are hard at work, seeking to "deceive the very elect" (Matthew 24:24). As we abide in Christ and in His truth, we shall be able to stand against the false teachers and their lies.

If we are truly born of the Spirit, the best attack we can make on false teaching is to bear witness to Jesus Christ the Son of God. We should not waste valuable time condemning those who teach error. Certainly we need to expose their error, but it is more important that we present the Son of God to a dying world. This is our calling. Paul declared, "But we preach Christ crucified, unto the Jews a stumblingblock, and unto the Greeks foolishness; but unto them which are called, both Jews and Greeks, Christ the power of God, and the wisdom of God" (1 Corinthians 1:23-24). Paul proclaimed Jesus Christ to all people. We must do the same, for it is Christ whom they need so that they can know the Father.

Not only does the Holy Spirit live within the believer, He is also our teacher. "But the anointing which ye have received in Him abideth in you, and ye need not that any man teach you: but as the same anointing teacheth you of all things, and is truth, and is no lie, and even as it hath taught you, ye shall abide in Him." This is not to suggest that we ignore men of God who have been called of the Lord to teach the Scriptures. God has His chosen ones, who have the gift of teaching, those whom God has called to be "pastors and teachers" (Ephesians 4:11). What John is saying is, if the only teacher you find available is not teaching the truth of God's Word, you should not listen to him. If you cannot find a true teacher of the Word, you still have the Holy Spirit, who is the greatest teacher of all. He will never lie to you like the false teachers.

In our day the Lord has made many tools available for the teaching of His people. With good Christian books, records, tapes, radio, and television, there are no limits to the possibilities for God's people to learn the truth from faithful servants. In many of our cities and towns, there are godly men who are exercising the gift of teaching in their pulpits, building up the saints in the Word week after week. How thankful we can be for the opportunities that are ours.

On the other hand, there are many areas in the world where there is very little good, solid Bible teaching. We who know the truth and possess the truth must do our part to use every means available to keep the truth of the Scriptures going forth to every part of the world.

The apostle calls upon the "little children" again: "Abide in Him; that, when He shall appear, we may have confidence, and not be ashamed before Him at His coming." Though there are some who depart from Christ, true believers "abide in Him." To "abide in Him" suggests more than to follow Him. It is to depend on Him for everything. As we do, we shall be fruitful for God. Our Lord said, "Abide in Me, and I in you. As the branch cannot bear fruit of itself, except it abide in the vine; no more can ye, except ye abide in Me. I am the vine, ye are the branches: he that abideth in Me, and I in him, the same bringeth forth much fruit: for without Me ye can do nothing" (John 15:4-5). If we who know Christ could only realize how weak we are in the flesh, and how important it is that we draw on Christ's strength for everything. We are completely helpless without Him. If we are really abiding in Him, we shall not look to ourselves but trust Christ wholeheartedly, realizing that we "can do all things through" Him (Phillipians 4:13).

A pastor was trying to persuade a young woman to teach a Sunday school class. Even though she was qualified and had adequate time, she declined with the excuse, "I don't want to be tied down."

"Do you recall," asked the preacher, "that in prayer meeting last week you wanted to be out and out for Jesus Christ, a true, devoted follower? If you were sincere in giving such allegiance to the Saviour who was *nailed down* on the cross for you, shouldn't you be willing to be *tied down* in service for Him?"

A look of shame came on the young woman's face as she said, "I see what you mean."

Why is it important that we be busy for God? "When He shall appear, we may have confidence, and not be ashamed before Him at His coming." Christ will return. Before He ascended from this earth, His word to His followers was, "Occupy till I come" (Luke 19:13). He did not tell us when He would return; He just simply said He would return. We are to be occupied with Him and all that concerns Him. This involves not only dedicated service, but holy living.

Without a holy life, service for God is meaningless. Thus John returns to a theme he stresses repeatedly in this Epistle. "If ye know that He is righteous, ye know that every one that doeth righteousness is born of Him." One of the marks of the false teachers John wrote about was their inconsistency of life. True believers are like

Christ in everything. They don't teach one way and live another. They follow their Lord in a life of holiness, proving their eternal relationship to Him. Is this true in your life? Do you prove your faith by a consistent walk?

3

DISTINCTION

> Behold, what manner of love the Father hath bestowed upon us, that we should be called the sons of God: therefore the world knoweth us not, because it knew Him not. Beloved, now are we the sons of God, and it doth not yet appear what we shall be: but we know that, when He shall appear, we shall be like Him; for we shall see Him as He is. And every man that hath this hope in Him purifieth himself, even as He is pure (1 John 3:1-3).

John has exhorted us to abide in Christ, resist false teaching, and live in anticipation of Christ's return. This combination seems to follow the pattern of the teaching of Scripture in general. Usually, whenever there is a reference to the return of Christ, there is an appeal for holy living. With the expectancy of Christ's return before us, we should live like children of the King.

When John the Baptist was busily engaged in his ministry of baptism, suddenly, in the midst of it all, he saw the Son of God approaching. With great fervency, he exclaimed, "*Behold* the Lamb of God, which taketh away the sin of the world" (John 1:29).

The Apostle John was no less enthusiastic: "Behold, what manner of love the Father hath bestowed upon us, that we should be called the sons of God." As I thought on this beautiful truth, I had to lay aside my work for awhile just to think on the magnitude of God's great love. There is nothing in all of life more magnificient than this thrilling truth. We, who are in Christ, were "children of wrath," deserving nothing but hell, but God, in His mercy, transformed us to become "children of light" with the eternal assurance of Heaven. Small wonder that John had to cry out in ecstasy, "Behold, what manner of love."

"What manner of " means "from whence did it come?" Where did this love originate? It is obvious that it is foreign to human flesh; it is an exotic love, coming not from the earth, but originating from another source. The Scriptures tell us that it comes from God, the eternal and all-merciful Creator of the universe. It is He who transforms a sinful unbeliever into a holy and worshiping saint.

The Apostle Paul in simplistic terms tells us how one may have this thrilling experience. "God commendeth His love toward us, in that, while we were yet sinners, Christ died for us" (Romans 5:8). When we believe on Christ, "the love of God is shed abroad in our hearts by the Holy Ghost" (Romans 5:5). Oh, what mercy! Immediately, upon believing on Christ, God in the person of the Holy Spirit makes His abode with us.

One would think that, after an undeserving sinner experienced this love, he would never desire to turn to the old paths of sin again. The thought of what God did for him through Christ ought to be enough to keep him walking with the Lord until he meets Him face to face. But this is not always the case.

David, like John, realized the wonders of this love as he considered his own wickedness in contrast to God's mercy and forgiveness: "He hath not dealt with us after our sins; nor rewarded us according to our iniquities. For as the heaven is high above the earth, so great is His mercy toward them that fear Him. As far as the east is from the west, so far hath He removed our transgressions from us. Like as a father pitieth his children, so the Lord pitieth them that fear Him. For He knoweth our frame; He remembereth that we are dust. As for man, his days are as grass: as a flower of the field, so he flourisheth. For the wind passeth over it, and it is gone; and the place thereof shall know it no more. But the mercy of the LORD is from everlasting to everlasting upon them that fear Him, and His righteousness unto children's children; to such as keep His covenant, and to those that remember His commandments to do them" (Psalm 103:10-18). Everyone who has experienced new life in Christ, can certainly relate to this.

A Christian tells of his father, who was fatally ill.

"As I watched the precious life ebbing away, I was overcome with remorse at the thought of the many times that I must have grieved that loving heart with my careless ingratitude and thoughtless disobedience. Penitently I begged his forgiveness for my wrongdoings in the past.

"I can't remember that you ever did anything wrong," my father said.

"I had expected instant forgiveness, but was not prepared for the full measure of pardon which I received. My father could not remember my wrongs because of his great love for me. How like the Heavenly Father's love for us." He says, "For I will be merciful to their unrighteousness, and their sins and their iniquities will I remember no more" (Hebrews 8:12).

The Father "bestowed" His love upon us. "Bestowed" reminds us of the fact that God's love is a gift. There is no possible way to buy or earn it. Furthermore, "bestowed" means that the gift can never be recalled. It is a once and forever bestowal, making it ours forever.

The climax of this marvelous truth is seen in the fact "that we should be called the sons of God." It is really "children of God." "Sons" is not one of John's words. That belongs to Paul, who spoke frequently of believers as "sons" who were "adopted," or placed into the family of God as full-grown children of God. John's word is "children," meaning born ones, those who have experienced the new birth and entered into the covenant privileges belonging to God's children.

The result of the new birth experience should be that the children of God will evidence the righteous nature of God. "If ye know that He is righteous, ye know that every one that doeth righteousness is born of Him" (John 2:29). "Children of God" live differently than "children of wrath." Basically, they desire to please the Father and do His will.

This has always been an enigma to the unsaved. They can't figure out how a person who went with them to places of disrepute, who did sinful things, can be changed suddenly and no longer desire this kind of life. Thus, John says, "the world knoweth us not, because it knew Him not." In other words, the unsaved cannot understand what has happened because they don't know the Lord. They try to reason divine truth with a natural mind. This is an impossibility. Paul says, "The natural man receiveth not the things of the Spirit of God: for they are foolishness unto him: neither can he know them, because they are spiritually discerned" (1 Corinthians 2:14).

The only possible way anyone can understand spiritual truth is to be spiritually minded. This is why it becomes so difficult for the child of God to fit into a godless society. Christ did not promise that because one is a

Christian he will naturally get along well with everyone. In fact, He taught just the opposite: "Think not that I am come to send peace on earth: I came not to send peace, but a sword" (Matthew 10:34). A sword divides, and very often the sword of God's Word creates divisions. This is not to suggest that Christians should be antagonistic or unsympathetic. We are also told, "If it be possible, as much as lieth in you, live peaceably with all men" (Romans 12:18). If we are misunderstood by the unsaved people of the world, we should not be surprised because the same was true of our Lord when He was here on earth. This ultimately led to His rejection and crucifixion. Thus, we may be sure that "the world knoweth us not, because it knew Him not."

Emerging from the glorious truth of God's great love, John says, "Beloved, now are we the sons of God, and it doth not yet appear what we shall be: but we know that, when He shall appear, we shall be like Him; for we shall see Him as He is." Please note that it is not, "We *shall* be sons of God." The truth is clear, "*Now are we* the sons of God." The very moment one believes, he is declared by God to be a son forever. There is no such promise for those who do not trust Christ. But if a person has truly received the Lord, he is born into the family of God by the Holy Spirit, and from that time forth and forever, he is one of God's dear children. "But as many as received Him, to them gave He power to become the sons of God, even to them that believe on His name" (John 1:12).

A Christian friend tells of witnessing to a man, who declared that it is impossible for a person to know he is saved until after he dies. "Life is like an examination," he said. "No one will ever know if he has 'passed' until he dies and faces God." Immediately, my friend showed him John 5:24 where Jesus said, "Verily, verily, I say unto you, he that heareth My Word, and believeth on Him that sent Me, hath everlasting life, and shall not come into condemnation; but *is passed* from death unto life." There can be no question about it, those who believe are passed immediately from death unto eternal life.

Becoming a child of God is wonderful enough, but there is still more to come, for "it doth not yet appear what we shall be." This does not mean that the believer is not knowledgeable about his future. There are scores of verses in the Bible revealing many details about things to come. What is meant here is that, though we have not yet seen these things with the physical eye, someday we shall. "It is written, Eye hath not seen, nor ear heard, neither have entered into the heart of man, the things which God hath prepared for them that love Him. But God hath revealed them unto us by His Spirit: for the Spirit searcheth all things, yea, the deep things of God" (1 Corinthians 2:9-10). Though we have knowledge of many of our spiritual blessings in Christ, someday they will be a present reality.

When will that time be? "When He shall appear, we shall be like Him; for we shall see Him as He is." The time is clear—at the return of Jesus Christ.

Several things should be noticed here. One is that John was certain that Christ would reappear. He says with unquestionable certainty, "He shall appear." No one need ever wonder about this. "The Lord Himself shall descend from heaven with a shout, with the voice of the archangel, and with the trump of God: and the dead in Christ shall rise first: then we which are alive and remain shall be caught up together with them in the clouds, to meet the Lord in the air: and so shall we ever be with the Lord" (1 Thessalonians 4:16-17).

Followers of Christ have had some wonderful times of fellowship together in churches, Bible conferences, home Bible classes, and many other places. But there is a meeting coming that will excel them all. Believers in Christ, both dead and alive, will meet Christ in the air to be with Him forever.

Oftentimes life becomes extremely difficult even for the most devoted believer. Sorrow and heartbreak become almost unbearable. But it will not always be this way for the best is yet to come. "For now we see through a glass, darkly; but then face to face: now I know in part; but then shall I know even as also I am known" (1 Corinthians 13:12). Some of us are surrounded by perplexing trials that confuse and disturb us. It is as though we are looking into a clouded glass. We cannot see the clear image; we are confused, even wondering "why?" Rest assured, the time is coming when we shall see clearly. Everything will become meaningful. All our questions will be answered when we see Jesus.

Can you think of anything more wonderful than seeing Jesus? We have sung about Him, talked about Him, studied about Him, communicated with Him, but the grand climax will be when we see Him. Every believer will be granted this privilege when Christ returns for His own. A glorious change will take place in us and then we shall see Him. We shall be like Him in that our sinful flesh will be changed completely so that we shall no longer desire sin. Temptation's appeals will never again affect us. We shall be glorified, like our Lord. All our tears will be gone. Never again will we experience sorrow from the burdens of life.

Indeed, the Christian has a marvelous future. New life begins at the cross. Daily it is empowered by Christ's presence. But the grand climax can only be known when we are caught up to meet Him in the air. What a day that will be, for from that time on we shall "ever be with the Lord" (1 Thessalonians 4:17).

The return of Christ for His people is not only a consoling truth for our encouragement, but a challenging impetus for our obedience. "And every man that hath this hope in Him purifieth himself, even as He is pure." "Hope" expresses the idea of confidence, or assurance. When Christ appears and we are glorified, we shall be sinless. But we need to heed the truth of Scripture now, and permit Christ to control us and live through us. The things which appeal to the worldly-wise should no longer be part of our program. When we see Him, we shall be transformed into His perfect likeness, but the purifying process ought to be evident in our lives every day.

Repeatedly throughout the Scriptures, the return of Christ is presented as a motive for consistent Christian living. "We have also a more sure word of prophecy; whereunto ye do well that ye take heed, as unto a light that shineth in a dark place, until the day dawn, and the day star arise in your hearts" (2 Peter 1:19). In some translations, "dark" is rendered as squalid or murky, meaning dirty. The verse is not referring to the darkness that results from the removal or the obscuring of the light, but the darkness that is caused by the foul dust or fog of earth. The same idea is expressed in Revelation 9:2, "And the sun and the air were darkened by reason of the smoke of the pit." There is a darkness in the world, which is the result of sin. This darkness encompasses all of us. It appears to be getting darker by each passing generation. Those of us who are in Christ are to shine as lights in the midst of darkness. If we, in any way, participate in the darkness of this world, our light will be clouded and our witness will be ineffectual. Consequently, how essential it is for believers in Christ to break with all known sin and let their light shine brightly for God "until the day dawn, and the day star arise in your hearts" (2 Peter 1:19). The Lord Jesus said, "Let your light so shine before men, that they may see your good works, and glorify your Father which is in heaven" (Matthew 5:16). We are to be light-bearers for God. If our lives are marred by sin, we shall have little effect on the darkness.

"For the grace of God that bringeth salvation hath appeared to all men, teaching us that, denying ungodliness and worldly lusts, we should live soberly, righteously, and godly, in this present world; looking for that blessed hope, and the glorious appearing of the great God and our Saviour Jesus Christ" (Titus 2:11-13). As we can readily see from these verses, the return of Christ is the "blessed hope." As wonderful as this marvelous event will be, it is more than that. It is a transforming hope that motivates us to follow God and do His will.

Though there may be differences of opinion among God's people concerning some of the details in connection with Christ's return, there should be perfect unanimity about the unquestionable fact of His return. Long ago, the angels declared at our Lord's ascension, "This same Jesus, which is taken up from you into heaven, shall so come in like manner as ye have seen Him go into heaven" (Acts 1:11). Since the return of Christ is a conclusive fact in Scripture, we who are in Christ must not only believe it but live each day in preparation for the return of the King of kings.

Are you looking for Christ's return? If you are, is the purity of Christ evident in you? Let the Lord have full possession. Give Him complete control. In humble obedience to His will, tell Him that you want Him to be Lord of all. Don't try to do in your own strength what

He alone can do. He said "Without Me ye can do nothing" (John 15:5). Submit to His Lordship and enjoy His endless blessing.

DIFFERENTIATION

Whosoever committeth sin transgresseth also the law: for sin is the transgression of the law. And ye know that He was manifested to take away our sins; and in Him is no sin. Whosoever abideth in Him sinneth not: whosoever sinneth hath not seen Him, neither known Him. Little children, let no man deceive you: he that doeth righteousness is righteous, even as He is righteous. He that committeth sin is of the devil; for the devil sinneth from the beginning. For this purpose the Son of God was manifested, that He might destroy the works of the devil. Whosoever is born of God doth not commit sin; for His seed remaineth in him: and he cannot sin, because he is born of God. In this the children of God are manifest, and the children of the devil: whosoever doeth not righteousness is not of God, neither he that loveth not his brother (1 John 3:4-10).

"Whosoever committeth sin transgresseth also the law: for sin is the transgression of the law." The latter part of this verse could also be translated, "sin is *lawlessness*." Actually, sin is self-rule as opposed to God's rule. All sin evidences selfishness. In a refusal to submit to God's desires, the selfish heart seeks its own will. In the case of the believer, it is the response to the dictates of the old nature rather than the new. This, God declares to be lawlessness or rebellion.

God's people need not be controlled by the old nature: Christ "was manifested to take away our sins; and in Him is no sin." Though we are not sinless, victory is available through Christ. It was achieved when our Lord died on the cross and rose again. As the result, the very moment one receives Christ, he receives a new nature which desires holiness. The old nature, however, will not give in easily. Usually, a struggle ensues.

Dr. Clarence Macartney used to depict the two natures by telling of a visit he made to an art museum. While there, he saw a statue illustrating the words of Victor Hugo, "I feel two men struggling within me." Out of a block of marble, two figures were emerging. One was bestial, fierce, cruel, sensual. The other was striving desperately to get free; it was refined, noble, spiritual, intellectual. Dr. Macartney said, "This is a study for which any one of us might sit as a model."

The two natures are opposites and are at enmity with each other constantly. "The flesh lusteth against the Spirit, and the Spirit against the flesh: and these are contrary the one to the other: so that ye cannot do the things that ye would" (Galatians 5:17).

Surely, every believer is aware of the two natures within and their resistance to each other. If we have received Christ, we should understand that He "was manifested to take away our sins," making possible all the power needed to follow in the way of the new nature, and to live in Christ's victory. "Likewise reckon ye also yourselves to be dead indeed unto sin, but alive unto God through Jesus Christ our Lord" (Romans 6:11).

When Christ died on the cross, we who have received Him, died with Him. We need to "reckon," that is, *think* on this monumental truth. Though the old nature was not supplanted by the new, we need not be subservient to the old because of our death and resurrection with Christ. Having risen with Him, we are the recipients of His resurrection power. For this reason, there is never a time when we cannot overcome any sin. In Christ, it is not beyond us to "lay aside every weight, and the sin which doth so easily beset us" (Hebrews 12:1).

Have you experienced the reality of the assuring truth that Christ "was manifested to take away our sins"? Or are you still bogged down with the evil desires of your sinful flesh? Why suffer in defeat when Christ wants you to be happy in His victory?

There lived a Bible teacher who, all his life, had been known for his quick temper. It could flare up in an instant. One day this believer came to the realization that his old self actually died on the cross and that the Holy Spirit was within him, willing to take control. Embracing this fact in all of its reality, he became a changed man. He had such a transformation that some of his friends wondered if even by trying they could get him mad. The words of Galatians 2:20 became meaningful in his life in a very practical way. "I am crucified with Christ: nevertheless I live; yet not I, but Christ liveth in me: and the life which I now live in the flesh I live by the faith of the Son of God, who loved me, and gave Himself for me."

The same could be true in the life of every believer. We need only realize that we are dead in Christ, and then, trust Him to live through us.

Don't look for an improvement of the flesh for it can never get any better. It is the crucifixion of the flesh that is important, so the Holy Spirit can take charge. Then it will truly be "Christ in you, the hope of glory" (Colossians 1:27).

Sin is one of the criteria for determining the verity of

one's profession of faith in Christ: "Whosoever abideth in Him sinneth not: whosoever sinneth hath not seen Him, neither known Him." If a believer continues to live in known sin, irrespective of what he says about his conversion experience, this verse makes it plain that he has never really met the Lord. Thus we may conclude that how one lives following his professed conversion indicates whether or not he is really saved.

The word "abideth," expresses the idea of steadiness, without vacillation. The keeping power of Christ is evidenced in the believer's life as he walks with his Lord consistently. He is not zealous for God now and lukewarm later. He "abides" in the Lord.

The result of "abiding" in the Lord is that the child of God will not follow in the old paths of sin. "Sinneth not" means that he will not habitually practice sin. Though the old nature continues to be active, the power of Christ is greater. There is no suggestion here that the believer will not or cannot sin following conversion. John did not believe in sinless perfection. This is clear from the first two chapters of this Epistle. He realized that Christians could and would sin. But he also knew that true believers would not practice sin habitually.

It is the transformed life that proves our relationship to Christ. "He that saith he abideth in Him ought himself also so to walk, even as He walked" (1 John 2:6). "By their fruits ye shall know them" (Matthew 7:20). *What* we are proves *whose* we are.

"Little children, let no man deceive you: he that doeth righteousness is righteous, even as He is righteous." We are not to strive to produce our own righteousness in an attempt to be like Christ. Not only would this be extremely frustrating, but impossible. Righteousness is the gift of God. God "hath made [Christ] to be sin for us, who knew no sin; that we might be *made the righteousness* of God in Him" (2 Corinthians 5:21). At the moment of conversion, we are "made" righteous in Christ. We are the possessors of the righteousness of Him who is altogether righteous. Any goodness we have is not ours, but Christ's. We have been made righteous by the supernatural power and grace of God.

The unsaved have no power to live righteously, for they have only a sinful nature. Even though they may do things that appear to be good, it is but a false attempt of sinful flesh to be righteous. The unsaved cannot experience victory over sin, for they are children of Satan, who is the instigator of sin. Some feel that it is rather harsh to speak of the unsaved as children of the devil. We must face reality. "He that committeth sin *is of the devil*; for the devil sinneth from the beginning."

When Jesus was confronted by some of the unsaved leaders in His day, who had condemned Him, He declared, "Ye are of your father the devil, and the lusts of your father ye will do. He was a murderer from the beginning, and abode not in the truth, because there is no truth in him. When he speaketh a lie, he speaketh of his own: for he is a liar, and father of it" (John 8:44). The devil's "own" includes anyone who has never received Jesus Christ as Saviour and Lord. Regardless of their church membership, their philanthropy, or attempts to do good, they are children of the devil and, as the result, under the condemnation of God.

No one need remain in such a state, however, it was "for this purpose the Son of God was manifested, that He might destroy the works of the devil." Because of Christ's death and resurrection, anyone can be delivered from Satan's bondage. The sinner need not be bound to his sins: "if the Son therefore shall make you free, ye shall be free indeed" (John 8:36). The homosexual, the prostitute, the selfish miser, the liar, the cheat, all can find immediate deliverance through Christ. The gospel "is the power of God unto salvation to *every one* that believeth" (Romans 1:16). There are no exclusions. Anyone who is willing to believe that Jesus Christ is the Son of God, that He died on the cross for sin and rose again, can be eternally saved and delivered from the power of sin.

"The Son of God was manifested, that He might destroy the works of the devil." "Destroy" as used here, does not mean to destroy in the sense of abolish. Rather, it is to *break up*, or *to give deliverance from*. When Christ returns to rule and reign on earth for a thousand years, Satan will be bound during that time. Following this reign, Satan will be judged and cast into the lake of fire. He and his works will be destroyed forever. But presently, he "as a roaring lion, walketh about, seeking whom he may devour" (1 Peter 5:8). Even so, as far as the believer is concerned, Satan's power is limited. For this reason, no believer can ever say, "I cannot stop sinning." We have been delivered from Satan's power.

We must never forget that our strength to overcome temptation and sin is in Christ. We cannot trust ourselves for a moment. Though we received power to overcome sin at conversion, we must look to Christ constantly to give us the continual victory. We cannot trust in our conversion experience but in the Christ of conversion. The novelty of the experience may wear off and the joy and enthusiasm disappear, but if our full confidence is in the Lord, we have nothing to fear. Jesus Christ is Lord!

In the next several verses, John continues along the same line as the previous verses, although his presentation is a little different and more complete. "Whosoever is born of God doth not commit sin; for His seed remaineth in him: and he cannot sin, because he is born of God." "Commit" expresses the idea already discussed of continuing in sin. Sin in the believer's life should be the exception rather than the rule. The reason he does not continue in sin is that God's "seed remaineth in him." When he believes on Christ, he receives new life, the life of God. "A new heart also will I give you, and a new spirit will I put within you" (Ezekiel 36:26). It is Christ at work through the "new heart" that keeps the believer from sin. The things he formerly loved that appealed to his old nature should become distasteful. What makes this possible? The "seed" that "remaineth in him." No longer must he attempt to overcome temptation and sin in the energy of weak flesh. He has the power of God. As long as he depends on this power, "he cannot sin." As in verse 6, this is not to suggest that he is not able to sin. It means that through the power of Christ within, as he depends on this power, he is able not to sin. Sin is ever active in the believer, but it no longer reigns because he "is born of God." Having been born from above, he has been forgiven of all his sins and has become the recipient of power over sin.

Only a proportionate few of God's people seem to realize the mighty power we possess in Christ. If they did, many more Christians would not trifle with sin as they do. "Ponder the path of thy feet, and let all thy ways be established. Turn not to the right hand nor to the left: remove thy foot from evil" (Proverbs 4:26-27). If left to ourselves, it would be impossible to "remove thy foot from evil." But the Lord has given us unlimited power to do it. Though we have been delivered from Satan's stronghold, we need to remind ourselves repeatedly that this enemy has not given up on us. He is out to destroy every true believer. But we are "kept by the power of God" (1 Peter 1:5). At no time is it our power that overcomes the devil. Our only guarantee of continued victory is confident trust in the keeping power of the Lord Jesus Christ. If we daily, hourly, every moment, look to Jesus "the author and finisher of our faith," we need not sin. We have the promise that "sin shall not have dominion over you" (Romans 6:14). This truth can be appropriated only by complete and full submission to Christ's control.

"In this the children of God are manifest, and the children of the devil: whosoever doeth not righteousness is not of God, neither he that loveth not his brother." Thus, our subject is summarized: if one walks in the way of the Lord, he belongs to the Lord; if, on the other hand, he follows in the paths of wickedness, he belongs to the devil. Unless a person is exemplifying the Lord in a life of holiness and righteousness, he is not a member of the family of God.

Is Christ real in your life? Is He Lord of all? Are you experiencing victory over sin?

Senator Mark Hatfield has shared his experience, telling how he grew up in a home where the Bible and the church were taken for granted. "But," he said, "it was a religion of habit, not of commitment. I remember vividly the night in 1951 while I was sitting alone in my parents' home. For months, my words in the classroom as a teacher had been coming back to mock me. I was urging my students to stand up and be counted, but I was a very silent and a very comfortably seated Christian. That night, in the quiet of my room, the choice was suddenly made very clear. I could not continue to drift along as I had been doing, going to church because I had always gone, because everyone else went, because there wasn't any particular reason not to go. Either Christ was God, the Saviour and Lord, or He wasn't. And, if He were, then He had to have all my time, all my devotion, all my life. I made the choice that night."

Have you made the choice? If not, do it now, and then, let the power of God flow through you. Forsake your desires and ambitions, and choose only that which the Lord wants, Let it be true in your life that "it is God which worketh in you both to will and to do of His good pleasure" (Philippians 2:13). This is the happy life, the life of victory and blessing.

DISPOSITION

For this is the message that ye heard from the beginning, that we should love one another. Not as Cain, who was of that wicked one, and slew his brother. And wherefore slew he him? Because his own works were evil, and his brother's righteous. Marvel not, my brethren, if the world hate you. We know that we have passed from death unto life, because we love the brethren. He that loveth not his brother abideth in death. Whosoever hateth his brother is a murderer: and ye know that no murderer hath eternal life abiding in him (1 John 3:11-15).

The message of love is as old as the incarnate Christ, for "God is love" (1 John 4:16). Nine times in this brief Epistle, John uses the expression, "from the beginning." In contrast to the false teachers, he wanted us to know that what he wrote had been obtained from the only credible source.

Anything anyone has ever known about true love has come from God. There has never been a time in human history when He has not manifested love. As the result, all who are related to Him by faith in Christ are obligated to love in the same manner. As a matter of fact, the language used by John in verse 11 is emphatic: "we *should* love one another." Love is more than an option for the believer; it is his duty and obligation. Anything less than this is sin.

At conversion, the child of God not only receives a new nature, but a new disposition. Though he may have been hateful and unkind, this should change, for he is reborn to love. No longer should it be difficult for him to overlook petty unkindness, thoughtless deceit, unjust criticism, and spiteful retaliation. The love of Christ within is abundantly sufficient to overcome the hatred that surrounds him.

Who of us could begin to fathom the depths of God's love toward us? While playing on the living room floor, a little girl was asked by her mother, "How much do you love me, dear?" The child thought for a minute as she stared out the window into the star-studded sky, and exclaimed, "All the way from here to the stars and back again." That would only be a suggestion of what God's love is toward us. Having experienced this unchangeable love in Christ, we should love others, even as He loves us. Our Lord emphasized this emphatically when He said, "This is My commandment, That ye love one another, as I have loved you" (John 15:12).

Suppose all Christians were to do this. One thing is certain, never again would anyone hear of "divisions" or "splits" in Bible-believing churches. With all sincerity, we would practice the truth of Psalm 133:1, "Behold, how good and how pleasant it is for brethren to dwell together in unity!"

God's love is needed so greatly among believers these days. One can hardly find a church where the work is not being hindered by hatred, smoldering in the hearts of some of the members. Small cliques and factions often oppose whatever seems worth while. There are those who put little fences around themselves, and behind those fences they include only those who are congenial toward them, and agree with them at all times. Many churches have these invisible fences with little groups behind them. Need we wonder why we are not seeing God at work in many circles?

The story is told about the man who went into the business of raising ducks. He made a number of pens with strong fences around them, and into each pen he put a distinct breed of ducks. A mountain stream ran through his property and all went well until the spring floods came. The waters flooded the pens until soon the fences were covered and all the ducks were swimming around together.

One of the pressing needs in most churches is a mighty outpouring of God's Spirit so that Christians will be lifted above their fences and drawn together in the love of God. "For this is the message that ye heard from the beginning, that we should love one another."

Several years ago, while ministering the Word in Winnetka, Illinois, I saw these lines on a church bulletin board:

> In essentials: unity
> In nonessentials: liberty
> In differences: love
> In all things: Christ

If all of the Lord's people were to put these principles into practice, the effectiveness of the body of Christ would be increased tremendously.

In Romans 12:10, we are told to "Be kindly affectioned one to another with brotherly love; in honor preferring one another." As followers of Christ, we have no choice in the matter. We are indebted to manifest love; "we *should* love one another." Obedience to the commandment of love for the believer is as essential as "Thou shalt not steal," "Thou shalt not commit adultery," or any of the other commandments in the Scriptures. Some believers would consider it a horrible sin against God to break the aforementioned commandments. Yet, they fail to give consideration to their daily transgression of the commandment of love.

Give prayerful thought to the needs of your own heart and life in this respect. Don't dwell on the shortcomings of others. Examine yourself. Are you mastered by God's love or dominated by a selfish nature that is unloving and unkind? The hatred in your heart might be an index of the fact that you have never really come to Christ. If this is the case, you haven't yet experienced God's love. Respond to His love immediately, for He loves you with an everlasting love.

John has made his point; love for others is a positive proof of discipleship. Believers are to be zealous for God, honest and trustworthy, and actively engaged in serving the Lord, but the real test comes in the extent to which they manifest the love of God. "By this shall all men know that ye are My disciples, if ye have love one to another" (John 13:35).

Why is it so necessary that Christians be loving? Simply because it is through love that the lost are drawn to Christ. It is not logic or arguments, but God's love that melts hearts. Could it be that many are turned away from Christ because of a lack of love in Christians? When love is real enough, strong enough, and concerned enough to reach the lives of the lost for Christ, the barriers of unbelief will be destroyed.

There is another reason why believers should be filled with God's love. The apostle relates it as he tells us why Cain killed Abel. The believer is not to be "as Cain, who was of that wicked one, and slew his brother. And wherefore slew he him? Because his own works were evil, and his brother's righteous." Evil and righteousness are like oil and water; they never mix. Because Cain had not experienced the love of God, he was overcome by hatred. As the result, he became extremely jealous of his brother, Abel, and murdered him.

What a warning this should be to every believer. Cain "was of that wicked one." That is, he was influenced by the "pernicious one," who attempts to drag others down to the same destruction awaiting him. Satan is well aware of what the Scriptures say about his fate. But being "a murderer from the beginning," he refuses to give in. Thus he is busily engaged in garnering as many followers as possible. He plagues believers as well as unbelievers. Two of his well-used tools are hatred and jealousy. Satan has no respect for anyone; he uses these tools on everyone. Who of us has not been touched by them at some time, perhaps many times? Even when we were dwelling in the heavenly places, suddenly we found ourselves in the valley because of the hatred that bred jealousy. The wise man was right when he declared, "Jealousy is cruel as the grave" (Song of Solomon 8:6). It is a living death. Many a saint has become totally ineffective for God because of jealousy in his heart.

F. B. Meyer tells of a meeting at Keswick, England, at

which he was the first speaker. He spoke with much
restraint and finished his message with the feeling that
he had been unusually ineffective. He was somewhat
embarassed, especially when the next speaker ministered
with unusual freedom and power, in marked contrast to
Dr. Meyer's weakness.

The seeds of jealousy and resentment began to take
hold until, very quickly, Dr. Meyer was reminded by the
Holy Spirit that he must rise into victory, and with prayer
for his brother, rejoice in the fact that God was using
him. After an inward struggle, he was enabled to put his
whole heart into what the speaker was saying, as he
sincerely rejoiced in the glorious harvest that followed.

F. B. Meyer never forgot the opportune victory God
gave that night, which, at the same time, could have
meant horrible defeat in his service for Christ.

Regrettably, not all Christian servants have experienced this victory. Some are bound by the evil of
jealousy. Others have inward hate that robs them of
effectiveness.

Oh, child of God, let Jesus Christ master you. There
is no hatred or jealousy in Him. Rejoice when others are
exalted above you, even though you may think you are
more deserving. Paul wrote, "I thank my God always
on your behalf, *for the grace of God which is given you*
by Jesus Christ (1 Corinthians 1:4). Most of us find it
easy to thank God for the grace we have received for
ourselves, but it is not always easy to thank Him for the
grace He gives to others. Does it disturb you to see
someone else being blessed of the Lord in something you
think you can do better? If so, you haven't yet entered
into the fullness of God's love. Can you pray with joy
and thanksgiving for those who seem to have greater
gifts and are being used more extensively than you? If

you can, this is a good indication that you have experienced the fullness of God's love.

Because one is mastered by God's love is not to suggest that he will never again be confronted by the Cain-spirit. John warns us, "Marvel not, my brethren, if the world hate you." "The world" has reference to the unsaved, who have not experienced the love that was "from the beginning." Sometimes, as they observe the blessing of the Lord in believers' lives, they become very jealous, and express their hatred in various ways. Realizing this, God's people should not expect to escape unkind treatment from the people of the world. As long as man has existed, the spirit of Cain, which is really the spirit of Satan, has been exercised by the unsaved, resulting in hatred and persecution toward those who know and love the Lord. John reminds us that we are not to be surprised if we receive this kind of treatment from those who do not love Christ.

We who belong to the Lord cannot control the way the unsaved treat us, but we are responsible for how we respond. We must be extremely careful lest we become revengeful. Our Lord gave instructions as to how we should react under such circumstances: "Blessed are ye, when men shall revile you, and persecute you, and shall say all manner of evil against you falsely, for My sake. Rejoice, and be exceeding glad: for great is your reward in heaven: for so persecuted they the prophets which were before you" (Matthew 5:11-12). We must never feel sorry for ourselves, thinking we are being treated unfairly. Rather, we should "rejoice" in the fact that Jesus is Lord and He has everything under control. Regardless of what unsaved people do to us, we must show forth God's love. This is the only way we shall be able to convince them God's love is real and necessary.

Some years ago, Charles Starkweather and his girl friend went on a bloody rampage, committing eleven murders in Nebraska and Wyoming. Later, the two were caught and placed behind bars. At the trial, the girl's father was heard to say, "If she is found guilty, it is I who should be sentenced, for I did not give her the love a father should."

Many a father has failed to give love to his children, but our Father in Heaven has never failed to share His love with anyone who was willing to receive it. God's love knows no resentment or hate. It reaches out to everyone: "God commendeth His love toward us, in that, while we were yet sinners, Christ died for us" (Romans 5:8).

How do unbelievers come to know and experience God's love? Very often it is through those of us who have been born again. We are God-appointed ambassadors of love. Is His love recognizable in you? Maybe you say you are a Christian, and yet there is hatred in your heart. This is to one's spiritual life what cancer is to the body. Experience the deliverance God has for you. Know the joy that comes through the freedom that only Christ gives. Surrender your heart and life to Him. Let Him fill you with His love.

The apostle reiterates his thought of love as a convincing proof of one's relationship to Christ: "We know that we have passed from death unto life, because we love the brethren. He that loveth not his brother abideth in death." When a believer has love for other believers, there need be no question about his salvation. But if he professes to be a follower of Christ while being resentful and hateful, we have good reason to wonder. Without a disposition to love, it is doubtful that he has experienced new life in Christ. Love is a crucial test of conversion.

Notice that the verse does not read, "We know that we have passed from death unto life, because we believe all the fundamentals of the faith; or, we work for God; or, we give to the church liberally; or, we read our Bibles and pray every day; or, we attend church every Sunday." It doesn't say anything about these things, as important as they are. It says, "We know that we have passed from death unto life, because *we love the brethren*."

You will observe also that it does not say we love *some* of the brethren. We love *all* the brethren. The word used for "brethren" means *children of one family*. Believers, who are in fellowship with God, will love all those who are in the family of God.

When selfish Lot became resentful of Abraham and his plans, Abraham reminded him of an important truth: "we be brethren" (Genesis 13:8). This is something we must not forget, for we belong to each other in the family of God. Strife should be unheard of among those who love the Lord.

An elderly native on the mission field, who had only recently been converted from cannibalism, was speaking to a group of Christians. He began his message by saying, "Brethren," and then he paused. "That's a new name, isn't it? We didn't know the meaning of that word in our heathenism. It is the gospel of Jesus Christ that has taught us the meaning of brethren."

How needful that all Christians know the meaning of "brethren." We are told that "one is your Master, even Christ; and all ye are brethren" (Matthew 23:8). The distinguishing characteristic of brethren is that they ought to love one another. If they do not, from what John tells us, they are not brethren. Regardless of what they say or do, if they do not have love for each other, they negate their profession.

Why is it such a serious matter when a professing believer fails in his obligation of love? For the reason that "whosoever hateth his brother is a murderer." Not only is one who does not love the brethren "abiding in death," but even worse, he is considered a murderer. It is obvious from the Scriptures that hatred results in spiritual manslaughter which, in the eyes of God, is as serious as physical manslaughter: "no murderer hath eternal life abiding in him." This is not to suggest that a murderer cannot be saved. If he were to believe on the Lord Jesus, the Lord would save him and he would no longer be considered a murderer, for God would forgive him. As a child of God, he could be delivered from the hatred in his heart. But as long as hatred continues in a person's heart, Christ refuses to live there.

As you doubtless realize, hatred is a serious evil that must be guarded against constantly. Whenever there is any trace of it, it should be confessed to the Lord immediately. Only Christ can give us victory over this instrument of the devil. Those of us who know the Lord should pray daily that God will fill us to overflowing with His love, that we shall have a sincere desire to manifest this fruit of righteousness to all.

It has been said that there was a strange tribe of natives in Africa, who had no method of counting. Someone asked one of them how many sheep he had. "I don't know," was his reply. "Then, how do you know if any are missing?" His answer was, "Not because the number would be less, but because of the face that I would miss." These natives did not know about arithmetic, but they knew about love and concern. They were not worried about numbers, but they were anxious about faces.

We need more of God's love so that we might overcome our selfishness and reach out into the lives of others.

Why not ask God at this moment to give you a new measure of His love. If there is any trace of hatred, claim the victory through Christ, our forgiving Lord.

DUPLICATION

Hereby perceive we the love of God, because He laid down His life for us: and we ought to lay down our lives for the brethren. But whoso hath this world's good, and seeth his brother have need, and shutteth up his bowels of compassion from him, how dwelleth the love of God in him? My little children, let us not love in word, neither in tongue; but in deed and in truth. And hereby we know that we are of the truth, and shall assure our hearts before Him. For if our heart condemn us, God is greater than our heart, and knoweth all things. Beloved, if our heart condemn us not, then have we confidence toward God. And whatsoever we ask, we receive of Him, because we keep His commandments, and do those things that are pleasing in His sight. And this is His commandment, that we should believe on the name of His Son Jesus Christ, and love one another, as He gave us commandment. And he that keepeth His commandments dwelleth in Him, and He in him. And hereby we know that He abideth in us, by the Spirit which He hath given us (1 John 3:16-24).

John is known as the apostle of love. This was not always the case, for there had been a time when he was one of the "sons of thunder" (Mark 3:17). With a heart burning with hatred, he wanted to invoke the judgment of God on the Samaritans (Luke 9:49-56). But the Lord performed a marvelous work of grace in the apostle's life, and his hatred became love. Following this experience, he recognized the value of God's love and had much to say about it.

Considering Christ's sacrificial love, we notice an important analogy: "Hereby perceive we the love of God, because He laid down His life for us: and we ought to lay down our lives for the brethren." The wonderful example of our selfless Lord is presented in contrast to the poor example of the selfish Cain. Thinking only of himself, and prompted by his jealous heart, Cain slew his brother Abel. But prompted by His great love, with no regard for Himself, our gracious Lord gave Himself to die on the cross for sinful humanity.

All who have trusted in Christ for salvation, should exemplify this same spirit of selfless sacrifice in their attitude toward others. The measurement of Christ's love for us was seen in the price He paid to deliver us from our sins. The measurement of our love for Him will be shown in the sacrifices we make to help fellow believers.

Only as we claim Christ's victory over the evil of the self-life can we ever hope to be useful for God. There has never been a selfish believer who has at the same time been fruitful. To be used by the Lord, one must have a sincere heart-love for people. Paul portrayed this divine love in 1 Corinthians 13, saying it "seeketh not her own." This love is always reaching out to help others, while giving little thought to selfish whims. All too few believers have come to this place of victory in Christ.

Many are like the little boy who was given seven cookies to share with his friend. Later, his mother said, "Frankie, I hope when you divided the seven cookies, you gave Joe four." "No, Mom," he replied, "I knew they wouldn't come out even, so I ate one before I began to divide them."

Few of us ever seem to overcome the tendency to interpret everything in the light of our own interest. But how different is the spirit of love that John is writing about. This love requires the sacrifice of self. "*We ought to lay down our lives for the brethren.*" There is a moral obligation here that cannot be overlooked. If we are followers of Christ, it is our responsibility to sacrifice for those whom He loves.

If one does not respond to the needs of his Christian brother, his relationship to Christ and His love is dubious: "But whoso hath this world's good, and seeth his brother have need, and shutteth up his bowels of compassion from him, how dwelleth the love of God in him?" If a believer who is having his needs met by God's gracious provision, knows of a Christian brother who is lacking in the essentials for life and welfare, he is obligated before God to offer sacrificial help. If the believer does not offer to provide help, he is shutting "up his bowels of compassion from him." This means that he is shutting the door of his heart tight to any feelings he might have toward helping the needy. It is obvious that such a person has never received new life in Christ, for newness in Christ results in selflessness, which leads to sacrifice. This is expressed so clearly by Paul, "And that He died for all, that they which live should not henceforth live unto themselves, but unto Him which died for them, and rose again" (2 Corinthians 5:15).

Becoming a Christian is more than saying, "I believe." It involves the commitment of one's entire life to Jesus as Lord. When this is done, self will be defeated, and sacrifice will be the result. "I," "my," "mine" will be forgotten and the will of God will be given priority. This is not to say that the Tempter will no longer appear to entice us through the old nature. Paul made it clear that the battle would be continuous, for the flesh does not give in easily: "But I keep under my body, and bring it into subjection" (1 Corinthians 9:27). This is to say, "I buffet my body, and bring it into bondage." God's servant decided that in the strength of Christ, he was not going to allow the self-life to win. As we study his Epistles, there is no question as to who won the battle. Jesus Christ was Lord of all in Paul's life, the proof being that from the moment of his conversion to the day of his death, he was always reaching out, regardless of the cost, to help others.

"Because He laid down His life for us," we have a responsibility "to lay down our lives for the brethren." How essential that every believer become involved. We can, as we depend upon Christ to live through us.

The Christian faith should be expressed, not only in words, but in works: "My little children, let us not love in word, neither in tongue; but in deed and in truth." Christianity in action, not Christianity in talk, is what basically advances the cause of Christ.

Of course, John is not saying there should never be a time for words. Surely, we realize the importance of speaking words of encouragement to those who are in need of help. But words, regardless of how comforting and helpful they are, should never be considered enough when a brother or sister is in need. There is usually some practical act of kindness that should be done.

The Apostle James instructed us to be "*doers* of the word" (James 1:22). This is for all believers, even though we may be busy in the service of the Lord. Faithfully studying and preparing to teach and preach is important as we honor Christ in our opportunities for service. But we must never be too busy to give a helping hand to someone in distress. All believers have a definite responsibility to "weep with them that weep" (Romans 12:15). All our teaching and preaching will have little effect, if we do not get under the load of the care and burdens of others. "Bear ye one another's burdens, and so fulfil the law of Christ" (Galatians 6:2). What "law" is spoken of here? It is the law of love that Jesus established for His people, the kind of love that results in action.

When W. E. Gladstone was facing one of the great crises of his political career in the English government, he sat one morning at 2:00 o'clock, writing the speech with which he hoped to win a great political victory in the House of Commons the next day. At that hour, his doorbell rang. When he answered it, there stood the mother of a poor, friendless, dying cripple who begged him to come and help her boy. Without hesitation, Gladstone left the preparation of his speech to spend the night with the dying boy. It was just before daylight that the boy closed his eyes for the last time. Minutes before, he made his decision to receive Christ, as the result of the love that had been expressed by the great leader, not only by word, but in "deed and in truth."

Gladstone, though tired in body, faced the day with confidence and peace. He was the happiest man in the world, for he had experienced the privilege of serving a young boy, in a tenement house, in the name of Jesus Christ. That day, he made the greatest speech of his life, carrying his cause to triumphant success.

God honors His faithful ones, who obey His Word in helping others, for when we help others we are really doing it for Christ: "Inasmuch as ye have done it unto one of the least of these My brethren, ye have done it unto Me" (Matthew 25:40).

There is a marvelous sense of confidence we receive in caring for the needs of others: "And hereby we know that we are of the truth, and shall assure our hearts before Him." To "assure our hearts before Him" is to experience the peace that results from obedience. In this, there is satisfaction and blessing unknown to the selfish heart.

For one to live for his own interests while ignoring the burdens of others, is to experience the restlessness which results from rebellion: "For if our heart condemn us, God is greater than our heart, and knoweth all things." When a person is selfish, his heart condemns him continually. He is devoid of inner peace. Though his conscience keeps prodding him to do what he should do, he refuses to heed the message and chooses what he wants above all else. However, there is a guilt feeling that plagues such a person. There is a tormenting sense of failure before God that cannot be escaped. This is one reason why some believers never seem to find the joy that others talk about. They are always striving, but never willing to meet the conditions.

But even worse than this is the fact that God is displeased. The conscience may be offended, but God is aware of the disobedience, for He "knoweth all things." It is bad enough for one to resist his conscience, but to live in resistance to God's desires is worse. Could it be that your heart is condemning you? Is there a sense of failure in your Christian life that you cannot fully explain? You read your Bible daily and pray as you should. You never miss church. You witness as the opportunities arise. You honor the Lord with your tithes and offerings. And yet, there seems to be a puzzling emptiness within. It is very possible that your heart is condemning you for not manifesting the love of God in living for others rather than yourself. You have been looking inward rather than outward. When you do look outward, it is through the glasses of selfishness. God knows all about this. He sees your heart as it is, and He longs for you to receive His victory. He loves you and wants to help you, but He cannot until you are willing. As we received salvation by faith, so we are to receive His will for our life. His will has to do with helping others. "Look not every man on his own things, but every man also on the things of others" (Philippians 2:4). When we put others before ourselves, we are close to the heart of God. This is the way our Lord lived when He was on this earth. We who follow Him should do the same. We can give no stronger argument for the cause of Christianity than this.

A missionary heard two natives talking about the Christians in his area. One said to the other, "What do you think of this new religion? Are you going to become a Christian, too?" "No," replied the other, "how could I? I have to think of myself, and these Christians are always thinking of others."

Wouldn't it be wonderful if all Christians were always thinking of others? It would certainly delight the heart of God. But obviously, we are not always thinking of others, and as the result, much that could be accomplished for Christ is being neglected.

When the believer is obedient to God, he experiences God's peace, for all is well between him and the Lord: "Beloved, if our heart condemn us not, then have we confidence toward God." No believer is perfect, but he can live in happy fellowship with the Lord. Desirous to please the Lord in everything, he seeks above all else to do the will of God.

There is an additional promise here for those who help their neighbor: "And whatsoever we ask, we receive of Him, because we keep His commandments, and do those things that are pleasing in His sight." Not only do we enjoy God's peace, but God's provision. When we get sacrificially concerned about the needs of others, we enjoy unusual prayer power and God cares for all our needs. Have you ever known of a believer who cared for the needs of others, who wanted for anything? I never have. We never shall, for this would be contrary to what God says in His Word. "The liberal soul shall be made fat: and he that watereth shall be watered also himself" (Proverbs 11:25). This is an axiom of God that really works. There are examples of its application all through the Word of God. In the New Testament, Jesus said, "Give, and it shall be given unto you; good measure, pressed down, and shaken together, and running over, shall men give into your bosom. For with the same measure that ye mete withal it shall be measured to you again" (Luke 6:38). When we help others with the right motive, we may be sure that we shall never lack any good thing.

God never fails. What He promises, He always does. Those who love and obey Him find this to be true.

"Whatsoever we ask, we receive of Him, because we keep His commandments, and do those things that are pleasing in His sight." Let any true believer meet the conditions for effectual prayer, and he will discover very quickly that this is true.

The mother of Tom Carter was a gracious woman, who lived for others. For many years, she prayed that God would save her son and use him to preach the gospel. But instead, Tom lived in wickedness and later, was imprisoned. His mother never gave up: she continued to pray believingly.

One day she received a telegram from the prison, informing her that her son was dead. The mother was stunned. She went to her room. Kneeling before God, and opening her Bible, she cried to the Lord, "Oh, God, I have believed the promises You gave me in Your Word. I believed that I would live to see Tom saved and preaching the gospel. Now I have this telegram telling me he is dead. Lord, which is true, the telegram or Your Word?"

She rose from her knees and wired the prison, saying, "There must be a mistake. My boy cannot be dead."

There *was* a mistake. The prison officials were extremely apologetic. Tom Carter was alive, and shortly after, he was saved. Upon being released from the prison, he became a preacher and a mighty soul winner. Indeed, we can trust God's Word with full confidence.

The keeping of God's commandments should especially concern two things: "And this is His commandment, that we should believe on the name of His Son Jesus Christ, and love one another, as He gave us commandment." Keep in mind, John is addressing the children of God here. In speaking of "believing," he has in mind the importance of trusting Christ completely for everything. If we have believed on Him for salvation and know that we are saved, then we must believe on Him for His provision today and every day. One does not receive Christ for salvation and then struggle through life the best way he can. He is privileged to depend upon the Lord all along the way, trusting Him for all his needs. Since the Lord has promised repeatedly throughout the Word that He will care for him, he never at any time has anything to fear. With perfect confidence, he must "walk by faith, not by sight" (2 Corinthians 5:7).

The other obligation John stresses is that we "love one another." It is of little value for the believer to trust

God for his own needs, if he is not faithful in caring for the needs of those around him. The two commandments John has stated go hand in hand. They are dependent on each other.

The chapter concludes with the assurance that "he that keepeth His commandments dwelleth in Him and He in him." Here is the harmony found in a congenial relationship with the Lord, which is the result of obedience. Nothing is more beautiful on this side of Heaven than for the believer to walk "in the light, as He is in the light." When this is the case, one's salvation need never be doubted for "we know that He abideth in us, by the Spirit which He hath given us." The indwelling Holy Spirit in the believer will keep before us the awareness of God along with the assurance of salvation. Oh, how wonderful to obey the Lord, to love Him, and to prove our love by reaching out of ourselves into the lives of others.

4

DETECTION

Beloved, believe not every spirit, but try the spirits whether they are of God: because many false prophets are gone out into the world. Hereby know ye the Spirit of God: every spirit that confesseth that Jesus Christ is come in the flesh is of God: and every spirit that confesseth not that Jesus Christ is come in the flesh is not of God: and this is that spirit of antichrist, whereof ye have heard that it should come; and even now already is it in the world. Ye are of God, little children, and have overcome them: because greater is He that is in you, than he that is in the world. They are of the world: therefore speak they of the world, and the world heareth them. We are of God: he that knoweth God heareth us; he that is not of God heareth not us. Hereby know we the spirit of truth, and the spirit of error (1 John 4:1-6).

After one believes on the Lord Jesus Christ, he is assured of the indwelling presence of "the Spirit which He hath given us." But there are also evil "spirits" in the world besides the Holy Spirit. The evil "spirits" are the motivating force behind the false prophets who propagate lies and error.

God's people need not fear these false prophets, however, for the Holy Spirit gives the wisdom and ability to distinguish truth from error. Without the Holy Spirit, this would be impossible. This is why many "good" church people have become the gullible followers of present-day cults; they have never received the Spirit through the new birth.

The apostle makes a sympathetic appeal to believers to be extremely careful what they believe. He uses the endearing term "beloved," as he makes his attack on the false teachers. As the apostle of love he reminds us that, in dealing with those who hold views contrary to the Scriptures, we should not be harsh and unkind, but must always manifest the love of God. We, who have experienced God's love through Christ, are obligated to reveal it to the false teachers when defending the truth.

A sound and worthwhile warning is given to believers: "Believe not every spirit, but try the spirits whether they are of God." We are not to believe everyone who claims that he has the truth, for he may be false, even demon possessed. Many thousands are being deceived by false teachers. The cults are thriving. Millions of dollars that should be going into the Lord's work to proclaim the gospel are being used to advance satanic error.

One of the reasons John wrote his first Epistle was to combat the false teaching that was driving its wedge into the church and deceiving the Lord's own. Since John's day, false teaching has multiplied in hundreds of shapes and forms. Error has advanced into extreme proportions. More than ever we must "try the spirits." Christian literature, religious broadcasts, and telecasts must all be analyzed and tested by God's Word. If what we read, hear, or see does not agree with the revelation of truth as we have it in the Scriptures, then it should be shunned, for it is false. We cannot take anyone or anything for granted. Because one speaks as a minister or a teacher of religion should not be accepted as sufficient evidence that what he says is true. If what he says and teaches coincides with God's Word, it can be accepted with gratitude. All else should be rejected as false.

Because of the subtlety of the false teachers, it is imperative that believers be diligent students of God's Word. Many, who have forsaken their churches to embrace the cults, failed in this responsibility. Having a shallow knowledge of the Scriptures, they were an easy mark for error. Not knowing the Bible, they readily embraced false teaching, believing it to be truth. Thus those who say they have received Christ should take time daily to read and study God's Word faithfully. Otherwise, they will become a target for the fiery darts of the wicked one.

Paul wrote, "Put on the whole armour of God, that ye may be able to stand against the wiles of the devil. For we wrestle not against flesh and blood, but against principalities, against powers, against the rulers of the darkness of this world, against spiritual wickedness in high places" (Ephesians 6:11-12). If we are going to stand against the powers of wickedness, we must use "the sword of the Spirit, which is the Word of God."

The president of a well-known Bible college tells of one of his students who had gotten into serious trouble. Previously, he had been brought before the authorities in the school for discipline. Finally he was brought to the president. After much discussion, the young student confessed his failure. In the course of the discussion, the president asked, "When did you last read your Bible?" The young man answered, "I have not read my Bible for a year."

If the child of God is to qualify himself to withstand false teaching, he must not only know the Scriptures, he must apply them to his life. The study of the Scriptures is one thing; the application is quite another. One does not mature in the faith because of what he knows about the Bible. There are some who seem to have a good grasp of scriptural truth, but they have remained as spiritual infants. It is the application of truth, in addition to a knowledge of it, that produces growth. God did not give us the Bible merely to teach us something, but to make us something. This means that the Bible must reach the heart, not simply the head. We must live what the Scriptures teach. Only then are we really in a position to "try the spirits." Apart from spiritual depth with Christ through a positive relationship to His Word, we are in a position to stumble and fall into error, as many believers have.

We have a conclusive test whereby the believer may distinguish truth from error: "Hereby know ye the Spirit of God: every spirit that confesseth that Jesus Christ is come in the flesh is of God." If a rightful place is given to the incarnation of Jesus Christ in what is being taught, it is obvious that it is Scriptural. No cult or false teacher would teach that the eternal Son of God left the glories of Heaven to be born of a virgin, to grow to manhood and die for the sins of all who believe. According to God's Word, those who believe and teach the incarnation pass the test of divine truth. Those who do not, fail. "And every spirit that confesseth not that Jesus Christ is come in the flesh is not of God: and this is that spirit of antichrist, whereof ye have heard that it should come; and even now already is it in the world."

In his Gospel, John recites the significant truth of the incarnation: "In the beginning was the Word, and the Word was with God, and the Word was God" (John 1:1). Further, "The Word was made flesh, and dwelt among us, (and we beheld His glory, the glory as of the only begotten of the Father,) full of grace and truth" (John 1:14). The incarnation is a fact of supreme importance.

There are several questions that should be asked when examining the credibility of doctrine. Is Jesus Christ the eternal Son of God? Did He enter this world by means of a virgin birth? Is He human as well as being very God? If these questions can be answered in the affirmative, there is strong evidence of truth. If not, it is probably satanic error.

"But when the fulness of the time was come, God sent forth His Son, made of a woman, made under the law, to redeem them that were under the law, that we might receive the adoption of sons: (Galatians 4:4-5). It was the plan of God that at the appointed moment of time, God's Son, who had inhabited eternity with the Father, should humble Himself and be clothed with a body of flesh to suffer for the sins of mankind, that all who believe on Him might be saved. This is a paramount truth of Scripture. Any denial of it is to classify one as an unbeliever. If Christ and the incarnation are not central, it is obvious that it is the "spirit of antichrist." It is against Christ and truth, and for this reason, those who are followers of the Lord should have nothing to do with it.

The birth of a child is an important event for all concerned. Every baby born has the potential of making a worthwhile contribution to life. But the birth of Jesus Christ exceeds every other in importance for He was born to be not merely *a* Saviour, but *the* Saviour. The world revolves around Him. History is divided by His birth. By His coming, men are divided into believers or unbelievers. While some have ruled their countries, Jesus Christ rules the universe. While man lives out his threescore and ten years on this earth and falls in death, Jesus Christ lives on throughout eternity. Many speak of Jesus as the great leader, the philosopher, the most unusual man who ever lived. But the Bible goes far beyond this. Jesus Christ is the Creator of the universe. He is the Giver and Sustainer of life. Apart from Him, men will die in their sins, and perish in hell. In Him, they will live forever.

Would you distinguish truth from error? Then consider the question, "What think ye of Christ?" What a person believes about Jesus Christ will provide the solution as to a true or false prophet.

A questionnaire was sent to fifteen hundred ministers, seeking their answers to a number of theological questions about their belief in a personal devil, angels, hell, and similar subjects. Of the questionnaires returned, eighty-nine per cent of the ministers said they did not believe in the supernatural virgin birth of Jesus Christ. If these ministers are representative of the pulpits of the United States, it is obvious that John 4:3 is being fulfilled before our eyes: "and this is that spirit of antichrist, whereof ye have heard that it should come; and even now already is it in the world."

Since Christ is the Son of God incarnate, we who are His followers should be committed to Him fully. Knowing that He is the eternal Son of God, who gave His life for us, demands that we who are in Him give our all for Him. "Other foundation can no man lay than that is laid, which is Jesus Christ" (1 Corinthians 3:11). Jesus is the bulwark of our faith. Everything we are and have depends upon our relationship to Him. Every moment of every day should be lived for His glory. "Whether therefore ye eat, or drink, or whatsoever ye do, do all to the glory of God" (1 Corinthians 10:31). This rules out selfish living. Jesus should be Lord. If He is, we shall prove it to the world by our manner of life.

Some years ago, a prisoner was released before his term expired because of his good behavior. The following Sunday, he went to church, and several Sundays later, he asked to be baptized. Delighted, the minister asked, "What was it in the message that brought you to this place of decision and commitment to Christ?" "It really wasn't anything you said, Sir," replied the prisoner. He explained that he had been in jail for a number of years because of the crimes he committed. "During those years," he said, "I watched many men who professed to be Christians. I was not too much impressed with most of them. But there was one man who was different. I watched him for five years. I never spoke to him, and he never spoke to me about his faith. Often I heard him speak for Christ. He was paroled before I was. When he was gone, I made up my mind that since that man was a real Christian, I could be one, too. I got down on my knees in my cell and asked Jesus Christ to come into my life as my Saviour and Lord."

Who of us can deny the importance of a dedicated life, lived consistently for Jesus Christ. It is our duty to tell others what we believe. Is your relationship to Christ such that wherever you go you create a thirst in the hearts of people for spiritual truth? How essential it is, since Christ lives in us, that we permit Him to live through us.

Though false teaching abounds on every hand, no true believer needs to succumb to it: "Ye are of God, little children, and have overcome them." The "little children" are literally the *little born-ones*. Having been born into the family of God through the Holy Spirit, believers have the mind of God as well as the indwelling presence of the Spirit. Thus, they "are of God"; they belong to Him;

they are His children. Never will they perish in hell. They are saved for eternity.

Because of their relationship to Jesus Christ, believers are in a position to detect false teaching, not because of their own intelligence but "because greater is He that is in you, than he that is in the world." The believer has the Holy Spirit within him to guide him into all truth. If he sincerely wants the truth, the Holy Spirit will make it evident to him.

The false teachers "are of the world," that is, they are of the present world system. All their ideas and teachings originate within the minds of men. Because the false teachers "are of the world: therefore speak they of the world, and the world heareth them." Usually what they teach is quite satisfying to the unregenerate. Since there is no need to change the life style, one can continue in the old ways of his sinful flesh. He can be religious without being inconvenienced. Being a part of the world system in which he lives, the teachings of the false teachers are plausible to him. As the result, numerous cults are thriving in our day, and experiencing a phenomenal growth.

There is no need for believers to be deceived by the false teachers for "we are of God." We have believed on Christ, and we have the Holy Spirit to guide us in the truth of the Scriptures.

The truth of God's Word is a divider of men: "He that knoweth God heareth us; he that is not of God heareth not us." Those who are true to the Word of God will desire fellowship with us in the truth. But the false teachers will readily reject our beliefs. They will scoff at the teaching of God's Word while continuing in their worldly philosophies.

Paul wrote to the Corinthians, "For the preaching of

the cross is to them that perish foolishness; but unto us which are saved it is the power of God" (1 Corinthians 1:18). The message of the cross is unreasonable to the false teachers, but to those who have experienced new life in Christ, it is a message of victory and blessing.

The Christian life has no room for compromise. It is a case of either being for Christ or against Him. This demands complete separation from unbelief. It is sad to see some of those who profess to be followers of Christ mingling with those who boldly assert error. The call is clear to all faithful believers: "Wherefore come out from among them, and be ye separate, saith the Lord, and touch not the unclean thing; and I will receive you, and will be a Father unto you, and ye shall be My sons and daughters, saith the Lord Almighty" (2 Corinthians 6:17-18). We, who love the Lord, are to be separated unto God while taking a faithful and bold stand against all that is false. "Watch ye, stand fast in the faith, quit you like men, be strong" (1 Corinthians 16:13).

DEVOTION

Beloved, let us love one another: for love is of God; and every one that loveth is born of God, and knoweth God. He that loveth not knoweth not God; for God is love. In this was manifested the love of God toward us, because that God sent His only begotten Son into the world, that we might live through Him. Herein is love, not that we loved God, but that He loved us, and sent His Son to be the propitiation for our sins. Beloved, if God so loved us, we ought also to love one another. No man hath seen God at any time. If we love one another, God dwelleth in us, and His love is perfected in us (1 John 4:7-12).

Realizing the subtle tactics of our ever-present enemy, one would think that the followers of Christ would unite in their common cause to proclaim the truth and resist false teaching. Regrettably, such is not the case. The family of God is divided into hundreds of segments, many seeking to advance their own fancies and whims. But God's plan still holds good: "Behold, how good and how pleasant it is for brethren to dwell together in unity" (Psalm 133:1).

Foreseeing the divisions that would arise, the Holy Spirit prompted the Apostle John to emphasize strongly the necessity of love, that true believers might be bound together in one body in defense of the truth, sincerely devoted to each other as brothers and sisters in Christ.

Known as the apostle of love, John begins this section of the Epistle with a word of endearment: "Beloved." What a word this is. Even the sound of it suggests that all animosity, jealousy and dislike be banished from the body of Christ. "Let us love one another." Though pertinent in John's day, doubtless this exhortation is needed even more in our day.

A little boy, upon returning from his first day in kindergarten, was asked by his mother what he learned. His reply was, "We learned to play with kids we don't like."

Probably this is one of the most significant lessons this child will ever learn. If he learned it well, it will be of extreme value to him all the days of his life. Would it not be advisable for some of our believers to return to kindergarten! They have not yet learned this invaluable lesson of how to love those they don't like.

Is it really possible for a believer to love everyone? In God's strength, yes, because "love is of God." Every believer receives the gift of God's love at the time of his conversion: "The love of God is shed abroad in our hearts by the Holy Ghost which is given unto us" (Romans 5:5). If love were of our own making, it is understandable why we might fail. But "love is of God." Our wonderful Lord is the source of love. He pours it out to His people, not to be stored up like a treasure but to be used in all our relationships with each other.

Twice before in this Epistle John has stressed the fact that love is a strong proof of one's relationship to Christ. Again he returns to this thought: "Every man that loveth is born of God, and knoweth God. He that loveth not knoweth not God; for God is love." No one can truly love Christ who is at enmity with his neighbor. If one says he is a believer while bearing a grudge of some kind, he would do well to examine himself carefully to see whether his profession is real.

When I was a pastor, I emphasized this fact in one of our Sunday morning services. At the conclusion of the message, I gave an invitation for any unsaved present to come forward to receive Christ. One of our active members came forward. My first thought was that possibly she had misunderstood the invitation, for she had been a faithful worker in the church for years and gave every evidence of being a Christian. While we waited for others to come, she stood at the altar sobbing, as the tears dripped from her cheeks. Following the benediction, I turned to her and asked, "Why did you come forward? What decision are you making?" Quickly, she replied, "I came forward to be saved. My life has been a sham. I have merely gone through the motions. This morning, for the first time, I realized that my hatred for another woman had closed my door to Heaven. I want to experience God's love through Christ so that I might reveal His love to the one I have despised for years." God wrought a wonderful miracle that morning. Hate was mastered by the love of Christ.

Several times John has declared that "God is love." The Bible teaches that God is other things as well, but we are assured that His nature is always love. This can never be changed.

Only a God of love could do what He did for each of us: "In this was manifested the love of God toward us, because that God sent His only begotten Son into the world, that we might live through Him." True love demands an expression; it must be proven. God the Father proved His love for us through the giving of His Son to die for our sins.

The end result of our Lord's supreme sacrifice was that "we might live through Him." When Christ becomes a reality in our life, the same love that made possible His sacrifice will enable us to live in a manner that will truly honor Him. Like Christ, we shall love not only the lovely but the unlovely. Even though He was aware of the sordid lives of many of those He confronted, because of His great love, He readily forgave them and cleansed them from sin. He has done this for all believers, and desires to do it for everyone. Those who have received Christ must love in the same manner He loves. This is possible only as we "live through Him."

Do you recall the instance when the writer of this Epistle called for fire from Heaven to consume the Samaritans? Yet later he became the apostle of love.

What happened? He permitted Christ to live through him.

Consider the Apostle Paul before his conversion, "breathing out threatenings and slaughter." The church feared this unscrupulous persecutor who appeared to be under the control of Satan. But the Spirit of the Lord opened his eyes to the truth, and he who hated Christians became one of them. Later, he wrote 1 Corinthians 13, the magnificent presentation of the power and effect of the love of God.

Peter, on the eve of our Lord's crucifixion, became so angry that he attempted to murder one of his Lord's would-be persecutors. Waving his sword in the air, he struck at his head, but missed his mark and cut off the man's ear. Reading Peter's Epistles, one is aware that he experienced a miraculous change. "Wherefore laying aside all malice, and all guile, and hypocrisies, and envies, and all evil speakings, as newborn babes, desire the sincere milk of the word, that ye may grow thereby: if so be ye have tasted that the Lord is gracious" (1 Peter 2:1-3). Peter surrendered to Christ and discovered the reality of what it was like to "live through Him."

Christ's love knows no measure or limits to those who "live through Him." Left to the control of ourselves and sinful flesh, we shall fail miserably. But if we depend on Christ completely, all traces of hatred can be removed permanently.

We have our prayer meetings when we remember the needs of our local fellowship, our faithful missionaries, and the sick and sorrowing. Would it not be well to put our need for love at the top of the list? There are many who pray together, yet they cannot get along together. Surely there would be a greater working of the Holy Spirit in our prayer meetings were we to be united in the oneness of Christ's love.

Several generations ago, there lived a faithful man of God by the name of John Fawcett, who pastored a small congregation in Yorkshire, England. One Sunday he announced that he felt directed to accept a call to a more sizable work in London. Later he preached his farewell sermon. Several weeks afterward, as his furniture and belongings were being loaded on the six wagons that were being used for the move, practically his entire congregation of men, women, and children stood around the little house in tears. When Mrs. Fawcett saw this, she said to her husband, "John, I cannot bear this; I know not where to go." "Nor I," replied John. "Nor will we go. Unload the wagons and put everything back." John Fawcett informed the congregation in London that it would be impossible for him to come. He then wrote the words of the famous hymn:

> Blest be the tie that binds
> Our hearts in Christian love;
> The fellowship of kindred minds
> Is like to that above.

There has never been a time in the history of the church when we have not needed a greater measure of God's love. Usually we look to the other person and expect him to do something about it. How necessary that each believer examine his own heart frequently and pray, "Dear Lord, cleanse me of every trace of dislike and hatred and fill me with Your love." In addition, if there is any feeling of ill will toward another brother or sister in Christ, it would be well to discuss it and seek forgiveness. As long as there is any division or dissension among believers, the work of God will be hindered.

We must never overlook the price that was paid so that we might experience God's love. "Herein is love, not that we loved God, but that He loved us, and sent His Son to be the propitiation for our sins." Having been redeemed by the blood of Christ, we are God's ambassadors to bear the message of God's love to all the world. If we who are Christians are not mastered by Calvary's love, how can we expect to reach a lost world filled with hate? The gospel which has as its foundation the love of God, must be proclaimed in love.

When the Father sent a redeemer for our sins, He not only sent a Saviour; He "sent His only begotten Son." The word "begotten" should not be misconstrued to mean "a son who is born." Christ, like the Father, is without a beginning and end. Actually, Jesus as the "only begotten Son" was the *unique Son*. He was different from everyone else who ever existed or who ever will exist. Being eternal with the Father, He assumed a body of flesh to enter the world as a baby, to mature and grow by way of a normal development in order to lay down His life as the Sin-Bearer for all who believe. Those who trust in Him for salvation become children of God immediately. They experience the promise and provision of Romans 10:13: "For whosoever shall call upon the Name of the Lord shall be saved."

Some think our Lord's command to go "into all the world, and preach the gospel to every creature" is an appeal to enter the ministry or become a missionary. The vast majority of Christians do not recognize Christ's words as a personal call to each one of us to make Christ known to everyone. Because of this, we often hear it said that if we cannot go, we can send someone else in our place. Can we? God did not command us to be "senders"; we are to be "goers" and "doers." He is the "sender," not we.

As the result of our failure to go, the world has not yet been reached for Christ. Millions know nothing of the love of Christ. There are many pastors who are preaching evangelistic messages to their congregations Sunday after Sunday, while outside their church there are thousands who are spiritually ignorant and on their way to hell. How we need a new realization of the meaning of Christ's sacrifice. "Herein is love, not that we loved God, but that He loved us, and sent His Son to be the propitiation for our sins." What He did for us He did for our neighbors and everyone in the entire world. This is the significant truth of the love of God. It is His will that all might be saved and spend eternity with Him. We are the ones to bear this message. "Ye are my witnesses," God says (Isaiah 43:12). From the moment of our conversion until we see Christ face to face, we are to be witnesses for Him. Wherever we are, in the home, the church, the office, the factory, the school, the store, on the street, or any other place, we are God's witnesses to share the message of God's love and grace.

An unsaved woman was persuaded to attend a gathering of church women who were sewing for missionaries. She spent the entire afternoon with them. Later, when someone tried to win this woman to Christ, she was not interested. She said, "Forty women were at that sewing meeting; they talked for three hours about everything in the world they could think of. Much of it was light, frothy talk, without meaning. Never a word was spoken about Jesus Christ. Do you think I could believe that Christians love Christ when they never say a word about Him?"

These forty women overlooked the fact that they

were supposed to be witnesses for God. Many Christians are guilty of this same neglect. Repeatedly we need to remind ourselves of the message of love. "Herein is love, not that we loved God." We were interested in ourselves, not God. In fact, most of us were running from Him. But in spite of this, in His overwhelming love, He sought us out and saved us. Oh, what love! Millions in the world need to hear about this love. We must tell them.

MY HEART IS THINE

O Thou, the Christ who died for me
Bearing the shame of Calvary
While Heav'n withdrew and left Thee lone
Unmoved by cry and deepest groan;
My heart now melts in love and tears;
My sin no more shall give me fears;
I'll trust in Thee through all the years,
Nor fear the world with all its sneers.

O Jesus, Lord, my heart is Thine
I know, I know, that Thou art mine;
Thy love constrains and holds me fast,
I'll tell it out while life shall last.

I see a world which knows Thee not
All stained with sin and deepest blot;
I'll tell that Thou can'st cleanse each spot,
The Christ on Calvary forgot;
I'll sing Thy love and power to save,
To make us triumph o'er the grave,
And make us long to see Thy face,
Transformed by Thy redeeming grace.

William M. Carle

"If God so loved us, we ought also to love one another." We are loved *of* God; now we must love *for* God. There must be no room in our heart whatsoever for bitterness or revenge. If we have truly met Christ, we are His to love.

Do you know who the really successful Christians are? Maybe you are thinking "Those who read their Bibles every day and take time for prayer. Those who are faithful in attending the services of their church. Those who honor God with their tithe and offerings. Those who are busy serving the Lord and reaching the lost for Christ." Surely we would have to agree that all of these are important and necessary exercises for effective discipleship. But what are any of them without love? Unless we are mastered by the love of Christ, whatever we do will have little value.

Leonardo da Vinci had a bitter enemy whom he despised. He decided to paint the likeness of the man's face into one of his pictures. When he painted "The Last Supper," he portrayed his enemy as Judas. It was the kind of thing that many artists did at the time, and the scheme would have been a bitter blow to the man. But the cruelty of what he was doing depressed da Vinci, and when he tried to paint the face of Jesus, he simply could not get into the right spirit of mind for such a task. At last he realized that his vindictiveness not only made him unhappy but actually limited his skill. He painted out the face of Judas and dropped his foolish animosity, and then painted the face of Jesus with grace and effectiveness.

"No man hath seen God at any time." To some, this might appear to be a contradiction since we are told in the Scriptures that there were occasions when God appeared to men and talked with them face to face.

These were manifestations of God. God is a Spirit and cannot be seen at any time. There were times, however, when he assumed a visible form and communicated with humans. Since the cross, our Lord no longer reveals Himself in this way, but He does manifest Himself through His people in love. Those with whom we associate should see Him in the love that is shown through us. This will always be true when His love is "perfected in us." Are we careful to allow Christ's love to show through us? Are we taking the time to permit this love to be "perfected in us"?

Richard De Haan, of the Radio Bible Class, has shared a clipping someone sent to him. It was about a father and his young son. The father was seated at his desk, preparing to write checks for the month's bills. Suddenly, his son of twelve, rushed into the room and announced, "Say, Dad, this is your birthday. You're fifty-five years old, and I'm going to give you fifty-five kisses, one for each year." He began to make good on his word when his father exclaimed, "Oh, Andrew, don't do it now; I am too busy!" The boy's silence was noticeable and his eyes filled with tears. Apologetically the father said, "You can finish tomorrow."

The boy made no reply, but was unable to conceal his disappointment. With a grieved expression, he walked away quietly.

That same evening, the father said, "Come and finish the kisses now, Andrew." But Andrew either did not hear him, or was not in the mood, for he did not respond to the invitation.

Two months later, as the result of an accident, the boy drowned in a nearby river and was buried near a little village where he loved to spend his vacations.

The father now says, "If only I could tell him how

much I regret those thoughtless words I spoke, and could be assured that he understands and knows how much my heart is aching because of my unkind request, there would be no man in all this wide world so inexpressibly happy as the one who sits today and thinks how he prevented an act that love inspired, and grieved a little heart that was all tenderness and affection."

The painful regret of a failure to show forth love is rarely forgotten. If God's love is "perfected in us," let's show it by living it; then we shall have no regrets.

DETERMINATION

Hereby know we that we dwell in Him, and He in us, because He hath given us of His Spirit. And we have seen and do testify that the Father sent the Son to be the Saviour of the world. Whosoever shall confess that Jesus is the Son of God, God dwelleth in him, and he in God. And we have known and believed the love that God hath to us. God is love; and he that dwelleth in love dwelleth in God, and God in him (1 John 4:13-16).

One meaning of *determination* is to arrive at a conclusion after carefully analyzing all the facts. Since John outlived the other apostles, he had ample time and opportunity to make some valuable observations. Having lived with the Lord Jesus during His earthly ministry, and having watched closely the lives of His followers for years afterward, he was in a unique position to emphasize the assurance of salvation.

"Hereby know we that we dwell in Him, and He in us, because He hath given us of His Spirit." One need not speculate about his relationship to God. "We know" leaves no room for "we wonder." One may be as sure of his salvation as he is of being alive. If he has sincerely received Jesus Christ as his Lord, there is no room for doubt.

A Welch lady, while dying, was visited by her minister who asked quietly, "Sister, are you sinking?" She looked at him as if she could not believe he would ask such a question. She exclaimed, "Sinking! Did you ever know of a sinner to sink through a rock? If I had been standing on the sand, I might sink. But thank God, I am on the Rock of Ages, and there is no sinking there."

When one is in Christ, he stands on the Rock that can never sink. The Psalmist has said, "He brought me up also out of an horrible pit, out of the miry clay, and set my feet upon a rock, and established my goings" (Psalm 40:2). There is no sinking through that Rock, for we are "kept by the power of God" (1 Peter 1:5).

It is with certainty that John says, "Hereby know we that we dwell in Him, and He in us." God would have every believer understand this, for without this knowledge, there can be no real peace or satisfaction in the Christian life. If we *know* we are in Christ and He is in us, we can face any circumstance in life with confidence and assurance.

Irrespective of the teachings of Scripture, there are many believers who live a "hope so" kind of Christian life. They refuse to believe God and enter into the joy of *knowing* they are saved. Others feel as if they are saved sometimes, while at other times they are not sure.

Could one be happy in marriage without the certainty of his mate's love? To live year after year without being confident that he is truly loved could lead to serious problems. We who are in Christ are told repeatedly in the Scriptures that God loves us, and He proved it at Calvary.

There are two Greek words in the Bible that are translated "know." One means the knowledge that depends upon feeling, observation, or experience. The other rests upon authority. A little child learns that two and two equal four. As he grows older, his knowledge broadens. If he lives to be one hundred years old, two and two still equal four. This knowledge does not depend upon his feelings, observation, or experience; it is the result of authority. The word used by John is the knowledge that rests upon authority—God's Word. It is what is known as "absolute knowledge." "We know" because God said so. Thus, anyone who has sincerely received Christ as Saviour and Lord need never wonder about his salvation, for "hereby know we that we dwell in Him, and He in us."

Not only does the believer possess the assurance of salvation because of the authority of God's Word, he may be certain "because He hath given us of His Spirit." At the moment of conversion, the Holy Spirit enters the believer to become a permanent resident. Our Lord said, "And I will pray the Father, and He shall give you another Comforter, that He may abide with you for ever; even the Spirit of truth; whom the world cannot receive, because it seeth Him not, neither knoweth Him: but ye know Him; for He dwelleth with you, and shall be in you" (John 14:16-17). Later the Apostle Paul wrote, "The Spirit itself beareth witness with our spirit, that we are the children of God" (Romans 8:16). The Holy Spirit within confirms the fact that the believer is God's eternal possession.

Is there any possibility that the Spirit might depart from the believer? Not at all. "He hath given us of His Spirit." The word "given" refers to a gift from God, and under the New Covenant His gifts are never recalled. Consequently, when God sends His Spirit to indwell the believer, the Spirit is there to stay.

With such truth stated so clearly in the Scriptures, how can anyone doubt his salvation? We must take God at His Word. If you are prone to doubt, say in the words of Sidney Cox:

> Chosen by the Father,
> Purchased by the Son,
> Sealed with the Spirit,
> I'm His very own!

Here is another valuable evidence that one has met the Saviour: "And we have seen and do testify that the Father sent the Son to be the Saviour of the world." One who is truly a born-again child of God will "testify" to the fact that Christ was sent into the world by the Father to be the Saviour. Since Jesus Christ came into the world "to seek and to save that which was lost," the believer will want to share this great truth with everyone possible. For one to say he is a Christian, while having no desire to communicate the thrilling truth of God's wonderful salvation to others, is enough to create doubts. When one is sincerely saved, the Holy Spirit within will prompt him continually to "bear witness." Of course, it is possible to resist the Spirit and quench His efforts, but to do this results in a fruitless and miserable life.

Shortly after Frances Ridley Havergal became a Christian, she went away to school. Having just entered into the joys of everlasting life, she felt as though she wanted to tell the whole world about Christ and His saving love. She was confident that there would be many others at school rejoicing in the same assurance she possessed, but what a disappointment. As Miss Havergal shared Christ with the other girls, she found that not only were they unsaved, but they had little or no interest. At first, she was disappointed, and had the urge to flee from such an atmosphere. But realizing that this would be a great mistake, she prayed for love and boldly witnessed to the saving grace of her Lord. God used her in a marvelous way, as she prayerfully and sincerely told the girls in her school about the One she loved.

Though Frances Ridley Havergal has been in Heaven over one hundred years, she still testifies to many tens of thousands through her wonderful hymns we sing from our hymnals. These messages in song speak with authority of the reality of Christ and the assurance we may possess in Him. Indeed, it is true, a witnessing saint is an assured saint.

Next the apostle stresses the importance of one's commitment to Christ if he is to know the certainty of his salvation. Some people never seem quite sure of their salvation because of a faulty beginning in their profession of faith. Salvation is not only an act of God, devoid of human responsibility. It is often obscured by an "easy believism" that overlooks two important requisites— repentance and commitment. When Paul declared, "Christ liveth in me" (Galatians 2:20), he was testifying to this great experience. Before his conversion, he did as he pleased. But this changed completely after he was transformed on the Damascus highway. His immediate response was, "Lord, what wilt *Thou* have me to do?" (Acts 9:6) Not only did Paul turn from his sinfulness, he committed himself to Christ's control with a willingness to obey. Salvation is more than a mental acceptance of the Son of God: it is surrendering one's life to Jesus Christ as Lord and Master. Anyone who does this need not wonder about his salvation. He will know that "God dwelleth in him, and he in God."

An elderly lady received Christ late in life. There was no question about her conversion. Everyone knew that she was different, for wherever she went, she lived for God and talked of her Saviour. One day a friend said, "Granny, you seem to be pretty confident about this Saviour of yours. I wouldn't be too sure about it if I were you. Suppose the Lord should let you slip through His fingers?" With a broad smile Granny said, "Don't you worry about that! I am one of His fingers."

Are you sure you are a Christian? Can you give a clear-cut, affirmative answer to this question? Or must it be "I think I am," or "I hope so"? Did you undergo a change in your lifestyle after you declared faith in Jesus Christ as the Son of God? Was your experience with the Lord similar to that described by Paul in 2 Corinthians 5:17: "Therefore if any man be in Christ, he is a new creature: old things are passed away, behold all things are become new"? Have you discovered, as you daily read God's Word, that often there are new areas that need to be opened to the Lord's control? Is the Holy Spirit within you in control of things, or is He merely a guest? If you are truly converted, you are no longer as you once were. We are told to "put on the new man, which after God is created in righteousness and true holiness" (Ephesians 4:24). Has this happened in your life? If the change is not obvious, possibly you haven't met the Saviour. Your decision to believe on Christ may have been insincere or faulty.

One of our radio listeners phoned me from a city many miles from where I live, and inquired as to the possibility of coming for counsel. We arranged a time, and when he arrived we spent several hours together. My visitor was a young executive, successful in his field. Several years before, he had made a profession of faith in Christ, but his problem of alcohol had never been overcome. He seemed to be bothered by the fact that, since he had believed on Christ, the urge to drink continued. We offered several solutions but, as I had never had the problem personally, I suggested that we go and talk with a friend who had faced the same problem and gotten victory. We discussed the problem at length in my friend's office. Finally, he asked the young man to tell about his conversion. In describing his conversion, he stated that on a certain day he made a decision. My friend asked, "What decision did you make?" There was a long pause, and then tears, but no answer. Here was the real problem—a faulty conversion. It was questionable if he had really met the Lord.

There have been many faulty conversions that were interpreted as salvation. John makes it clear that "whosoever shall confess that Jesus is the Son of God, God dwelleth in him, and he in God." To "confess that Jesus is the Son of God," is more than merely accepting a fact of doctrine. It is receiving the person of Jesus Christ as Saviour and Lord, while giving Christ complete control of the life. When He is in control, deceit, unkindness, lust, and scores of other evils will be banished. It will not be the old life made over, nor the old advanced to a higher level. It will be a spiritual rebirth through the power of Christ.

It is obvious that many church members have never had this experience. If they made a decision, it was faulty, for their lives do not evidence the transforming power of Christ.

When Peter and John were tried before the accusing Sanhedrin, the rulers and elders "took knowledge of them, that they had been with Jesus." Here were two unlearned fishermen, with the smell of the sea on them, yet they were identified by the fragrance of the Rose of Sharon because Jesus was their Lord. Though the believer bears the physical characteristics of the people of this world, yet spiritually he should bear the characteristics of the Son of God. Anything less than this does not evidence scriptural salvation.

In 2 Peter 1:10, the apostle says to all professed believers in Christ, "Make your calling and election sure." In other words, we are to give convincing proof to everyone around us that we are children of God. It is not enough to say, "I believe." In the words of John the Baptist, we must "bring forth therefore fruits meet for repentance" (Matthew 3:8). We must provide a practical indication of a new life.

While traveling from one country to another in Europe the famous artist, Paul Gustave Dore suddenly realized that he had lost his passport. Being very anxious to cross the border the same day, he said to the guards, "I am very sorry, but I have lost my passport. I hope you will let me pass without it. All that I can tell you is that I am the artist, Dore." The guards smiled at each other and then one of them said, "Don't try to deceive us. Many people attempt to enter our country by saying that they are some distinguished person." But Dore pled with them to believe that he was actually who he was. At that point one of the guards said, "All right. If you are Dore, take this pencil and paper and sketch that group of people standing over there." In a matter of minutes, the sketch was done and handed to the guards; they were convinced immediately.

Every Christian should be living in a manner that everyone around will be convinced that he has experienced new life in Christ.

"And we have known and believed the love that God hath to us. God is love; and he that dwelleth in love dwelleth in God, and God in him." It is difficult for the apostle to keep silent about God's love, which he had found so meaningful in his own life. Notice that "we have known and believed." "Known" has to do with knowledge, while "believed" refers to an experience.

It appeared that the great pioneer missionary, David Livingstone, had been lost in the heart of Africa. Henry Stanley, an explorer and newsman, led a party in search for the missing Livingstone. After some time, the missionary was located, and Stanley stayed on and spent four months with him.

After returning home, Stanley said, "I went to Africa as prejudiced as the biggest atheist in London, but there came a long time for reflection. I saw this solitary old man there and asked myself, 'how on earth does he stay here? What is it that inspires him?' For months, I found myself wondering about the old man, carrying out all that was said in the Bible. Little by little, my sympathy was aroused. Seeing his piety, his gentleness, his zeal, his earnestness, I was converted by him, although he had not tried to do it."

What was it that struck so deeply into the heart of an unbeliever like Stanley? It was not Livingstone's preaching; it was the love of God that radiated from this genuine saint.

When one has believed on Christ and abounds in His love, he will not have to doubt his salvation. On the other hand, if there is bitterness and enmity in his heart, he has reason to doubt that he is related to God.

In the portion of Scripture we have considered, John has offered us five valid, definite ways the believer may be assured that he has been passed from death unto life! 1, the authority of God's Word (1 John 4:13); 2, the presence of the Holy Spirit in the life (verse 13); 3, the impelling desire to bear witness to Christ (verse 14); 4, one's sincere and wholehearted commitment to Christ (verse 15); 5, the outworking of God's love (verse 16).

How do *you* line up with these evidences of new life in Christ? Are you really a child of God? Do you have any doubts about it? Are you confident that what you profess is real? If you have any doubts whatsoever, there is no better time than now to do something about it.

Recognize the fact that you are a sinner and completely helpless to save yourself. It is impossible to recognize Christ as a necessity until we see our own personal need of Him. Realize also that God will exclude no one from salvation other than those who exclude themselves. When the self-righteous scribes and Pharisees complained of the Lord Jesus eating with publicans and sinners, He said, "They that are whole need not a physician, but they that are sick. . . . I am not come to call the righteous, but sinners to repentance" (Matthew 9:12-13).

The rich young ruler, who asked the Lord Jesus how to obtain eternal life, declared that he had observed all the commandments from his youth. But when he was told to go and sell all that he had and give to the poor, and then take up his cross and follow the Son of God, he went away sorrowful. He did not realize that he was breaking two of the most important commandments: failing to love the Lord with all his heart, and not loving his neighbor as himself.

When the Philippian jailer was aroused to his spiritual senses by an earthquake, he cried out, "What must I do to be saved?" Paul and Silas gave him the answer, "Believe on the Lord Jesus Christ, and thou shalt be saved." He believed and was saved immediately.

God offers salvation freely to "whosoever will," but unless one is willing to come of his own volition and receive Jesus Christ, the door to eternal life remains shut.

If you are willing to receive Jesus Christ, who shed His blood for your sins, you can be saved at this very moment and know it. Your life can be changed, and you can become a possessor of everlasting life with the absolute assurance of someday being with Christ forever.

DISTORTION

Herein is our love made perfect, that we may have boldness in the day of judgment: because as He is, so are we in this world. There is no fear in love; but perfect love casteth out fear: because fear hath torment. He that feareth is not made perfect in love. We love Him, because He first loved us. If a man say, I love God, and hateth his brother, he is a liar: for he that loveth not his brother whom he hath seen, how can he love God whom he hath not seen? And this commandment have we from Him, That he who loveth God love his brother also (1 John 4:17-21).

"Herein is our love made perfect, that we may have boldness in the day of judgment: because as He is, so are we in this world." "Our love" is really *the love which is with us*. This is not human love, but God's love. Human love can never be made perfect. But the love that is implanted in the believer at the time of conversion makes possible the immediate possession of God's perfect love. This is the love Paul wrote about in Romans 5:5: "The love of God is shed abroad in our hearts by the Holy Ghost which is given unto us." This love, which is perfected in the believer at conversion, will never change; it is always perfect.

Believers are not to strive to produce more love for their neighbors and friends. We already have perfect love. The only workable solution for our dislikes and hatred is full commitment to Christ. For it is not "our love," but His love at work in us that is meaningful. It is that exotic, matchless, unbounded love that sent Jesus Christ to the cross to die for our sins.

It is difficult for any of us to understand fully the magnitude of God's love, since it is unlike the spirit of the world in which we live. Only as we are committed unreservedly to Christ can we possibly have a grasp of the reality of God's love.

A faithful pastor, whom the Lord had used to reach scores of lives over the years, lay dying. Several of his friends were gathered around his bed with his family. One of them prayed that the Lord would not let him die, that he would allow him to serve a little longer. "Because," he said, "Lord, You know how he loves You."

At this point the pastor interrupted: "No, God knows better. It isn't my love for Him, it is His love for me that is so very important." He reminded them of the occasion when Mary and Martha sent their message to Jesus regarding their brother, who was sick. "This message was not 'Lord, he who lovest You,' but 'He whom Thou lovest is sick.' It is not my imperfect love, but His perfect love for me."

Because God's love is "made perfect" in us, "we may have boldness in the day of judgment." "Boldness" here has to do with *confidence*. As the believer anticipates his judgment at the judgment seat of Christ, he might become fearful. Recalling his failures and neglect since conversion, he might be prone to regret the consequences. But not only has the love of God been perfected in us, it has resulted in a confidence in the finished work of Jesus Christ that assures us that "there is therefore now no condemnation to them which are in Christ Jesus" (Romans 8:1). Since the penalty for our sins was suffered by Christ and our judgment was meted out at the cross, we need not fear the judgment seat of Christ.

It is difficult for any of us to fathom the love of Christ. Who could understand completely why He should die such a terrible death while we are allowed to escape and go free? Have you never thought, "Why should He do it for me?" There is only one answer to this question: love, God's "perfect love." It is this same love that is at work in us, sustaining us day by day as we realize how far short we have come of the glory of God.

It would seem from what we have seen already in this verse that there could not possibly be any more, but there is: "because as He is, so are we in this world." Shut your eyes for a minute or two and let your thoughts dwell on the perfect Son of God. The Bible tells us, He "knew no sin," He "did no sin," and "in Him there was no sin." Try to visualize Him as the One who always did the right thing: who spoke no evil: who never possessed a single wicked thought: who was always kind. Everything He did glorified the Father.

Now think of yourself: the unkind words, the un-clean thoughts, the inconsiderate deeds. What a contrast! The wonderful fact is that we need not dwell on the horrible picture of ourselves. We are indwelt by the perfect nature of Christ which was given to us when we repented and believed. As God looks at us, He doesn't see our sinful nature, but the perfect nature of His Son. For this reason, John says, "As He is, so are we in this world."

Lift your head high. In Christ, you belong to the King of kings. Don't think about how weak you are, for "as He is, so are we in this world." We are redeemed by the blood of the Lamb—new creatures in Christ, to live in His power to show forth His praise and glory. Don't exist as a spiritual pauper when God intends that you be a spiritual billionaire. Realize your high calling. As the result, "walk worthy of the Lord" (Colossians 1:10).

We are living in an exceedingly dirty and filthy world. No matter where we look, there is growing degradation and immorality. But as children of God, we must live in a manner that honors Christ, for "so are we in this world." This is God's standard. It is not beyond us, for the Christian has God's perfect love within him.

"There is no fear in love; but perfect love casteth out fear: because fear hath torment. He that feareth is not made perfect in love." Who of us has not been tor-mented by fear? There is fear of poverty, fear of failure, fear of what people might think or say, fear of old age, fear of sickness, fear of loneliness, fear of sin, fear of death, fear of hell; the list is endless. Fears do not originate with God, but are the products of our faithless lives. "God hath not given us the spirit of fear; but of power, and of love, and of a sound mind" (2 Timothy 1:7). In His "perfect love," God has provided the sure cure for fear. As one depends upon Christ and realizes His sufficiency for every need of life, fear need not be a torment to the believer. As we trust the Lord for everything, His Word will be a constant encouragement. God says, "Fear thou not; for I am with thee: be not dismayed; for I am thy God: I will strengthen thee; yea, I will help thee; yea, I will uphold thee with the right hand of My righteousness" (Isaiah 41:10). Satan tries to get us to doubt God in an attempt to destroy our faith. But we may claim God's "fear not" and keep moving forward in victory.

Through the perfect love of Christ, we are able to negate every fear that haunts the souls of men. Because of our eternal riches in Christ, poverty can never touch us. We may not have much of this world's wealth, and even though there are those who might look upon us as failures, the story is different in God's eyes. Don't be moved by "the fear of man [which casteth] a snare" (Proverbs 29:25). We are not eye pleasers; we are to please God.

Are you fearful of old age? Think of it as the anteroom of Heaven, the stepping-stone to glory for the people of God. No matter what trials may come in old age, God's Word never changes. He says, "I will never leave thee, nor forsake thee" (Hebrews 13:5).

Should I fear sickness? Not if I am trusting Him who is perfect love, for He permits sickness in the lives of His people that we might derive spiritual benefit from it. After all, our bodies belong to Him. He knows what is best for us.

Neither need we fear loneliness, for our Saviour has promised, "Lo, I am with you alway, even unto the end of the world" (Matthew 28:20).

In Christ, there need be no fear of death, for He has

conquered death for the believer. At the moment of conversion, we are delivered forever from the clutches of this enemy. Christ died "that through death He might destroy him that had the power of death, that is, the devil; and deliver them who through fear of death were all their lifetime subject to bondage" (Hebrews 2:14-15).

Praise God, Jesus Christ conquers fear and we must let Him conquer all our fears. He will do this as we trust in His "perfect love." "The fear of the LORD is the beginning of wisdom" (Proverbs 9:10). Some join the beginners' class, but that's about as far as they get. Soon after conversion, they return to their doubts and fail to trust. The apostle has said, "fear hath torment." As long as we allow satanic fears to disturb us, we shall never know the fullness of the blessing of walking with God. "He that feareth is not made perfect in love." We shall have knowledge of the love of Christ, but shall fail in experience.

There have been Christians who trusted Christ for security in life, but had underlying doubts about the future. Never forget that our God is a *living God*. Today He is whatever He was thousands upon thousands of years ago. He possesses the same sovereign power, the same saving love, the same ability, simply because He is the same living God: the unchanging One. What He is today He will be after you leave this earth. The promises you enjoy at this moment will be the same after you die, for God declared, "I am the LORD, I change not" (Malachi 3:6). If you have definitely received Jesus Christ as your Saviour and Lord, the "perfect love" you received when you were saved will be the same within you throughout eternity. If you have fears about your future after death, it behooves you to ask yourself, "Have I really met the Lord?" If there are any doubts, settle this immediately by inviting Christ to become your Lord. Then thank Him for His "perfect love" and trust Him for everything.

There is a practical aspect to the "perfect love" that should be meaningful in the life of every believer. This is where the breakdown often appears. I have chosen to call it the *distortion*. Believers, of all people, are supposed to be loving and kind, but sometimes just the opposite is true. All of us have been guilty at times of allowing the flesh to distort God's "perfect love."

Notice the basis for the believer's love: "We love Him, because He first loved us." "Him" does not appear in the early manuscripts. At first it might seem that something is lost by leaving "Him" out of the verse, but as we dwell on it, it is obvious that something is gained. Not only do "we love Him, because He first loved us,"but we are to love all those of His people who love Him in the same manner in which we love Him. "We love" because of the miracle He performed within us enabling us to love. Before we were saved, we were selfish and loved only ourselves. Since God's "perfect love" made it possible for us to overcome this selfish love, we are obligated to love everyone. In Christ we can do this not only in word but in a practical way.

I ministered the Word at a conference for children and young people in the Kentucky mountains. Before I spoke, in one of the evening meetings I was seated in the audience during the song service. A young lady, about fifteen, played an accordian solo that was appreciated by everyone because it was done so well. Very proudly the little boy next to me leaned over and said, "That's my sister." I replied, "You are very fortunate, for she seems to be a lovely Christian girl."

After the service, the girl and her mother were greeting

friends, and I told them what the younger brother had said. The mother turned to her daughter and said, "See? He does love you." Quickly the daughter retorted, "You would never know it at home!"

Doubtless there are many loved ones who can identify with this; we seem to have a kind of love for the home and another kind for outside the home. As far as God is concerned, there is only one kind of love, "perfect love." We who are in Christ love "because He first loved us." Think what we were when Christ found us. Even worse, think what we might be today had He not found us. We did not deserve to be loved, for in God's sight we were unlovely. But because of His selfless love, He reached out and drew us to Himself. We must allow this love to master us so that in all our circumstances of life we shall love others as God loves us.

Is our love real, or distorted? Here is the test: "If a man say, I love God, and hateth his brother, he is a liar: for he that loveth not his brother whom he hath seen, how can he love God whom he hath not seen?" Not only is this practical, but logical. For one to profess to love "God whom he hath not seen" is absurd if he cannot love those whom "he hath seen."

Love to the believer should be as real as faith and belief. For one to say he believes while not expressing God's love, makes him a liar. The moment one believes on Christ, he receives the gift of God's love. If this love is not expressed, it is doubtful that he ever received it.

In 1867 D. L. Moody was preaching in a large hall in Dublin. Following one of the services a young man who did not look over seventeen approached Moody and said he would like to go back to the States with him and preach the gospel. Not knowing him or his ability, Moody said he was undecided when he would be returning. The young man asked Moody if he would please let him know when he got ready to return. The request was ignored.

After arriving in Chicago, Moody got a letter informing him that the young man would be arriving in New York, and he would like to come and preach in Moody's church. The great evangelist wrote quickly and tried to discourage the young man from coming, but he came anyway. It seemed that there was no way to get rid of him. Since it was necessary for Moody to be away again, he talked it over with his church officers and, though they were not too enthused about allowing a stranger to preach, they decided to go ahead. Moody assured them that this would probably take care of the young man, and they wouldn't be bothered with him again.

Upon his return to Chicago, Moody received a great surprise. His wife was thrilled, as were all the people, at the unusual gift the young preacher had. Moody's wife said to her husband, "He preached a little different from what you do. He tells the people that God loves them. I think you will like him." She was right. The evangelist's doubts were soon forgotten as night after night he gave way to this young man to preach.

Every evening the young preacher used the same text, though his message was different. His only text was John 3:16, "For God so loved the world, that He gave His only begotten Son, that whosoever believeth in Him should not perish, but have everlasting life." The crowds grew larger each evening.

Moody confessed, "I could not keep back the tears. I didn't know God thought so much of me. It was wonderful to hear the way this young man brought out Scripture. He went from Genesis to Revelation and preached that in every age God loved the sinner. He showed us that it was love—love—love that brought Christ from Heaven, that made Him step from the throne to lift up this poor fallen world. It was glorious; each night the sermon seemed to get better. The whole church was on fire before the week was over. I have never forgotten those nights. I have preached a different gospel since, and I have had more power with God and man since then."

In closing those seven nights of preaching, the young preacher, Henry Moorhouse, said, "I have been trying to tell you how much God loves you, but this poor stammering tongue of mine will not let me. If I could ascend Jacob's ladder and ask Gabriel, who stands in the presence of the Almighty, to tell me how much love God the Father has for this poor lost world, all that Gabriel could say would be that 'God so loved the world, that He gave His only begotten Son, that whosoever believeth in Him should not perish, but have everlasting life.' "

The Lord had baptized Henry Moorhouse into a sense of the divine love, and it was this that touched hearts. It is said that on his deathbed, Henry Moorhouse turned to his crippled child and said, "God is love."

If ever there was a time when the Church of Jesus Christ needed a new understanding of the love of God, it is now. We have allowed our petty differences to break fellowship, to alienate dearest loved ones, to hinder the working of the Holy Spirit.

The last verse of the chapter confronts us with an unending obligation: "And this commandment have we from Him, that he who loveth God love his brother also." Bible reading, prayer, and witnessing, as important as they are, if done without an expression of the "perfect love" that God has implanted in our hearts, is meaningless and ineffectual. It is not how much we know about the Scriptures that will convince a lost and dying world of the need of the Saviour; but it is as John has stated in his Gospel: "By this shall all men know that ye are My disciples, if ye have love one to another" (John 13:35).

If you are a Christian, you are a possessor of God's love; do the members of your family know it? Do your neighbors know it? Have they seen it at work in and through you? The best way for all those around us to understand the love of God is to see it in action. Let God's love flow through you.

5

DOMINATION

Whosoever believeth that Jesus is the Christ is born of God: and every one that loveth Him that begat loveth him also that is begotten of Him. By this we know that we love the children of God, when we love God, and keep His commandments. For this is the love of God, that we keep His commandments: and His commandments are not grievous. For whatsoever is born of God overcometh the world: and this is the victory that overcometh the world, even our faith. Who is he that overcometh the world, but he that believeth that Jesus is the Son of God? (1 John 5:1-5)

God never intended that anyone be dominated by sin and defeat. Through Christ, His Son, He offers a sure and better way. Several basics are necessary, however, if one is to experience a life of victory and blessing.

Salvation is where it all begins. "Whosoever believeth that Jesus is the Christ is born of God." One enters into the family of God the instant he believes that "Jesus is the Christ." There is no other gate of entry.

Belief in Christ is more than giving intellectual assent to facts about Christ. It is to commit one's self to the control of Jesus as Lord while acknowledging Him to be the eternal Son of God. This belief acknowledges Christ's substitutionary death, resurrection, ascension, and return in glory.

163

Should you have questions about believing in someone you have never seen, this need not be a problem. There have been many people in history who have lived and died. We would not for a moment question the facts that have passed on to us about them because we have not seen them. Not only do we have the facts recorded in history and in the Word of God about Christ, we have the evidence of millions upon millions of the changed lives of those who have believed on Him.

There are dozens of reasons why everyone should believe on Christ, though there are no reasons why they should not believe on Him. After all, everyone believes in something. When one considers what some people believe in, it is astounding.

During the Second World War, Geoffrey Gorer made a study of superstition in England. He found that one person in three had his or her private piece of magic: the scarf of the favorite girl, a lucky penny, a cupid, a Mickey Mouse. Even crosses, prayer books, and Testaments were carried, not for reasons of piety, but for protection. Gorer discovered that four-fifths of the population read a horoscope every week. No less than one-half of the population had consulted a fortune-teller at some time or other.

What do these facts tell us? An amazing number of civilized people have adopted a view of the universe which can most properly be designated as magical. Multitudes believe that the future is arbitrarily predetermined, that evil can be averted by the use of certain devices, and that good can be secured by the same simple and convenient means.

Be assured, there is nothing magical about putting faith and trust in the Son of God. One need only to believe on Him to discover the way of happiness, which is unknown to those who have not believed. Thus, if one is to overcome the sin in his life and live victoriously in this present, Satan-controlled world system, the first requisite is belief in Jesus Christ.

Those who are born into God's family are given gifts. There can be no question about it, "the greatest of these is love" (1 Corinthians 13:13). God in His mercy shares the gift of His love with every true believer. In gratitude, the child of God should direct this gift toward God and his fellow man.

This brings us to the next basic for a life of victory and blessing. Our Lord said, "Thou shalt love the Lord thy God with all thy heart, and with all thy soul, and with all thy mind. . . . And . . . thou shalt love thy neighbor as thyself" (Matthew 22:37,39). The Apostle John realized the importance of this obligation. Thus he was constrained to write, "Every one that loveth Him that begat loveth him also that is begotten of Him."

It is deeply disturbing to realize how many believers profess to love God, and yet they are indifferent and unloving in their relationships with those whom the Lord loves. Such believers have not yet entered into a life of victory in Christ.

Suppose God were partial in expressing His love toward His people as some of His followers are. He plays no favorites. His heartfelt concern is the same toward everyone: "I have loved thee with an everlasting love" (Jeremiah 31:3). We who are "born of God" should love "him also that is begotten of Him." We need to pray daily that we shall evidence the love of God in such a way that we shall love everyone the same.

The late President Eisenhower was planning a visit to the humble home of his mother. She was a small, white-haired woman in her eighties, with a cheerful face. While she was waiting for her distinguished son to arrive, her neighbor, knowing of the visit, dropped by with a dish of Pennsylvania Dutch "puddin' meat" which she prepared especially for the homecoming. "You must be proud of your famous son," said the neighbor to Mrs. Eisenhower. With her usual calm attitude, the loving mother asked, "Which one?"

Usually a mother's love is the same for all her children. Rarely does she prefer one above another. This is what God's love is like. We who are His through Christ must manifest this same love as we reach out with concern and compassion to those about us. We cannot afford to dislike or hate anyone. Not only will such an attitude ruin our testimony for Christ, it will make us "of all men most miserable." To be dominated by hate rather than love is satanic.

No one would deny the fact that there are some people who are hard to love. But if Christ is in control, we can say with Paul; " I can do all things through Christ which strengtheneth me" (Philippians 4:13). God will give all the grace we need to love the unlovely.

A pastor tells about a man in his congregation named Joe Webb. The pastor did everything he could think of to try to love Joe, but he found the task just about impossible. Frustrated, one day he called at the office of one of his men, who had always impressed him as being deeply spiritual, to discuss the problem. Said the pastor, "I cannot possibly love Joe Webb, and it disturbs me." He went into detail about the matter as the friend listened attentively. Finally the friend said, "I understand, Pastor. But what we must realize is that the Lord Jesus loves him." Upon hearing that the pastor wanted to run out of the office. Later, as he walked home, he prayed along the way repeatedly, "Lord Jesus, You love

Joe Webb and I do not, but I ask You to give me love for that man."

When Joe came to church the following Sunday, the pastor had an attitude of love for him that he had never known before. He went to see Joe and confessed his hatred, asking for forgiveness. Joe admitted that his feelings had been the same toward the pastor. "But Pastor," said Joe, "if the Lord can do that for you, He can certainly do it for me." A bond of love was established between these two men that was never broken.

Some months later the pastor, who appeared well and strong, was preaching his Sunday morning sermon. Suddenly he dropped to the floor, as though dead. He had suffered a severe heart attack. For the many weeks following, during his recovery, Joe Webb became a willing slave to the pastor's family, to do all he possibly could to help.

God's love is sufficient, if only we let the Lord work in our lives. Let us ask for a practical understanding of this truth: "Every one that loveth Him that begat loveth him also that is begotten of Him."

In addition to *belief* and *love*, obedience is the third basic that will enable us to dominate the forces that would destroy our usefulness for God. "By this we know that we love the children of God, when we love God, and *keep His commandments.*" Have you noticed how these principles are intertwined? When one believes in Christ, he is born of God. When he is born of God, he loves God's people. He then proves his love for God's people by obeying the Lord.

The liberals would suggest that the essence of Christianity is to love one's neighbor. If there were no other verses in the Bible to show the inconsistency of such teaching, the few verses we are considering in this chapter would be enough. Before there can be love for our neighbor, there must be love for God. And before there can be love for God, there must be a "new birth." Furthermore, those who are born again and love God and their neighbor will obey the Lord according to His truth as taught in the Scriptures: "For this is the love of God, that we keep His commandments."

Love for God and obedience are inseparable. Let no one say, while living in disobedience to God's revealed Word, that he loves God. This cannot be, for it is impossible for one to love the Lord without obeying Him. The Lord Jesus repeatedly made this clear. He said, "Ye are my friends, *if ye do* whatsoever I command you" (John 15:14), and, "If ye love me, *keep my commandments*" (John 14:15).

When we love God wholeheartedly, and do what He says, the result will be blessing. Examine anyone's life, spoken about in the Scriptures, who realized the blessing of God. Was the blessing not experienced in an act of obedience? Consider your own relationship to the Lord. Compare those times when Christ was merely Saviour to you with the ones in which He was Lord of all. When did you receive the greater blessing? There can be no question. Can you imagine what it would be like if all who professed to love God were at all times obeying Him and doing His will? Surely the body of Christ would possess power unknown by any generation of Christians.

One of the old writers, O. L. King, tells how, as a boy of eight, he had his first taste of coconut, which created an intense appetite for more coconut. But since his family was very poor, this appetite went unsatisfied. Though poor, King had been reared on the truth of God. At the age of twelve, he received his first dime with the liberty of spending it any way he wanted. As he walked down Main Street, in anticipation of making his purchase, what did he see in a grocery store window but coconuts for ten cents apiece. His first inclination was to get one. But, having only a dime, he felt he should look further. Approaching the window of a drug store, he saw New Testaments for ten cents each. With some inward struggle, he decided on the New Testament. To be sure, this was not an easy decision for a boy of twelve.

O. L. King read and studied his New Testament faithfully. Later he offered himself to be a missionary and when God sent him to the mission field, where do you think the Lord placed him? The home that God had already arranged for him was in the midst of forty acres of waving coconut palms. Indeed, the Lord never fails to honor the obedient life.

There are believers who feel that it is difficult to be a Christian. Some even express the opinion that the price is too great to live a life of complete surrender to God. But John says, "For this is the love of God, that we keep his commandments: and His commandments *are not grievous*." "Grievous" means heavy or severe. In other words, under no circumstances does God ever require too much of us. It all reverts to the principle of love. Of course, the unsurrendered life, dominated by the flesh and the world, will find His commandments "grievous." But if we really love the Lord with a desire to obey Him, His commandments will not be "grievous."

There is no need for the child of God to live in defeat. "For whatsoever is born of God overcometh the world: and this is the victory that overcometh the world, even our faith." All who are reborn of God have overcoming power. Through the Holy Spirit, they can say "no" to temptation and sin of any kind. This is not to minimize the demonic forces that surround us in this present world system. Satan is "the god of this world" (2 Corinthians 4:4), who goes about "as a roaring lion . . . seeking whom he may devour" (1 Peter 5:8). When we consider that Satan is stronger and mightier than any of us, it would appear that the odds are against us. But God assures His followers that He "is able to do exceeding abundantly above all that we ask or think, according to the power that worketh in us" (Ephesians 3:20). Satan is a mighty enemy, but those who have been born of God have the inner power to defeat their enemy.

Could it be that this overcoming power is not evident in your life? If so, maybe you have neglected to use the key that unlocks the door to God's power. And what is the key? Faith! "This is the victory that overcometh the world, even our faith." This brings us to John's fourth principle which is necessary if the believer is to dominate evil. Without this principle, God tell us, "It is impossible to please Him" (Hebrews 11:6). Full confidence in the Lord is a requisite for victory in the Christian life. "Who is he that overcometh the world, but he that believeth that Jesus is the Son of God?"

It is interesting to note that the Apostle John uses the word "faith" only once in all of his writings. Could it be that he wants us to see that it is the *object* of faith that is of greater importance—not our weak and faulty faith. We need to recognize this fact in a day when there are those who appear to be making a fetish out of faith. They suggest that if blessing comes to one's life, it is because of his great faith. If it is missed it is because of his little faith. Our Lord revealed the unreasonableness of such teaching when He said, "If ye have faith as a grain of mustard seed, ye shall say unto this mountain, Remove hence to yonder place; and it shall remove; and nothing shall be impossible unto you" (Matthew

17:20). A grain of mustard seed is minutely small. One need not have great faith, but if it is genuine faith in the Son of God, things will happen. Especially will he experience "the victory that overcometh the world."

The word "overcometh" is in the present tense and means that the one who keeps continually exercising confidence in the Son of God, with complete dependence on Him, keeps overcoming the world. But the moment the believer looks to himself, things, or other people, he will fall in defeat. We live in human bodies with all the limitations of the flesh. The Christian, having been born of God, possesses victory in Christ that can enable him to overcome the flesh, but he must trust Christ for everything. If he does, there is no reason for him to be bogged down by fear, worry, lust, or any other evil when God has made such a provision available. Our problem is, however, that we fail to exercise complete confidence in the Lord.

Maybe you realize that there is a barrier in your life keeping you from God's victory. Don't try to sidestep it; don't worry about it. Face it in full dependence on the Lord. Be very sure that you are relying upon Him completely, for this is the essence of faith. Faith is not *what* we believe but *in whom* we believe. Paul declared, "I know *whom* I have believed." When one knows the Lord and trusts Him without restraint, he will experience the overcoming victory that dominates the world.

Be reminded again that this victory begins with belief; it is proven in love; it is achieved through obedience; and it is experienced by faith. It can be a moment-by-moment experience for every child of God as we rely upon the Lord Jesus and believe Him for everything.

The story is told of the little boy who was led to Christ one Sunday by his Sunday School teacher. She proceeded to point out the necessity of depending on Christ constantly for victory. Overjoyed, the little fellow practically ran all the way home after Sunday school to tell his father what happened. His father sought to discourage him by saying it was impossible to live the Christian life. "Oh, but Dad," said the boy "you don't understand. I have Jesus, and He'll help me to live for Him." The father shook his head and said, "No, son, it's not possible, not even for a week." "But what about a day?" asked the boy eagerly. "No," said the father, "not even for a day." There was silence for several minutes and then, hopefully, the boy said, "Well, what about a minute, Dad? Can't a person live the Christian life even for a minute?" The father thought and then said, "Well, I suppose it's possible for a minute." "Good!" said the little fellow. "I'll live for Him minute by minute!"

That's what the Christian life is all about. It is a minute-by-minute dependence on Jesus Christ. It is impossible for us to live the Christian life in our own strength, but with faithful dependence on the Son of God, He will live it through us. What a privilege we have as children of God. We have been born into the family of God. We have received God's love so that we can love everyone. He has given us the strength to obey His Word so we may "walk by faith, not by sight" (2 Corinthians 5:7). As we "walk by faith" we experience the power of God enabling us to dominate the world of sin and lust. Oh, child of God, enjoy your possessions in Christ. Do not limit Him by unbelief.

DEPICTION

This is He that came by water and blood, even Jesus Christ; not by water only, but by water and blood. And it is the Spirit that beareth witness, because the Spirit is truth. For there are three that bear record in heaven, the Father, the Word, and the Holy Ghost: and these three are one. And there are three that bear witness in earth, the spirit, and the water, and the blood: and these three agree in one. If we receive the witness of men, the witness of God is greater: for this is the witness of God which He hath testified of His Son. He that believeth on the Son of God hath the witness in himself: he that believeth not God hath made Him a liar; because he believeth not the record that God gave of His Son (1 John 5:6-10).

Three witnesses are presented that depict our Lord's position as the Son of God—the water, the blood, and the Spirit.

Because the teaching of the Corinthian Gnostics was becoming more widespread, the apostle was constrained to combat this error with the truth. It was being taught falsely that at the baptism of Jesus, the Divine Being of Christ came upon the human Jesus, but departed from Him prior to His crucifixion. John declared that the One who died on the cross was the same One who was baptized by John the Baptist; there was never a time of separation between Jesus and Christ. He always was and always will be Jesus Christ, the Eternal Son of God.

"This is He that came by water and blood, even Jesus Christ; not by water only, but by water and blood." The "water" refers to Christ's baptism at Bethabara, beyond Jordan. It was at this time that our Lord officially began His earthly ministry, not as a human, as the heretics taught, but as the God-Man who several years later died on the cross for the sins of the world. John the Baptist testified to Christ's deity: "I saw the Spirit descending from heaven like a dove, and it abode upon Him. And I knew Him not: but He that sent me to baptize with water, the same said unto me, Upon whom thou shalt see the Spirit descending, and remaining on Him, the same is He which baptizeth with the Holy Ghost. And I saw, and bare record that *this is the Son of God*" (John 1:32--34). There was no question in John the Baptist's mind. He knew he was baptizing Jesus Christ, the Son of the living God.

In addition to John the Baptist's testimony, God the Father also gave witness to Christ, as His Son, at the baptism: "And lo a voice from heaven, saying, This is My beloved Son, in whom I am well pleased" (Matthew 3:17). Consequently, in response to the false claims of the Gnostics, John substantiated the fact that our Saviour both began and ended His earthly ministry as Jesus Christ, who was both human and divine.

The facts of Christ's humanity and deity were not established "by water only, but by water *and blood*." Our Lord did not die a martyr's death. He was very God pouring out His life's blood to atone for sinful humanity.

It has been said that the blood of Christ was of greater value in His veins than when it was shed on the cross. This is not what the Bible says: "Forasmuch as ye know that ye were not redeemed with corruptible things, as silver and gold, from your vain conversation received by tradition from your fathers; but with the precious blood of Christ, as of a lamb without blemish and without spot" (1 Peter 1:18-19). The blood Christ shed at Calvary was "precious blood." It was precious because it was undefiled. It was offered as God's perfect sacrifice to atone for all sin. When the first Adam, the federal head of the human race, sinned, the bloodstream of humanity became defiled. From that moment on, each of us became "as an unclean thing, and all our righteousnesses are as filthy rags; and we all do fade as a leaf; and our iniquities, like the wind, have taken us away" (Isaiah 64:6). But He who declared that "the life of the flesh is in the blood," also said, "I have given it to you upon the altar to make an atonement for your souls: for it is the blood that maketh an atonement for the soul" (Leviticus 17:11). The cross was the altar where God made "an atonement for the soul" in the offering of the "precious blood" of His Son for the souls of all men.

Some years ago, a blood specimen was taken from an African national in Lagos, West Africa. As the result, ever since, millions of people all over the world have been protected from yellow fever. All of the yellow fever vaccine produced has been derived from this original strain of virus obtained from this one African. It has given immunity to millions of people in many countries.

To be saved from yellow fever, one must receive an application of the vaccine that originated from one man. To be saved from the judgment of God, one must receive an application of the unique precious blood that was shed by the Son of God alone.

The heretics of John's day saw Jesus as a mere man.

To them, He was a good man but frail flesh like all humans. There are many false teachers these days who preach this same kind of Jesus. But this is not the Christ of the Bible; this is a man-made savior who is weak and helpless. Those who hold such a view of the Son of God are still blinded by their sins, having never seen the light.

For many years, a big lump of something, supposedly a stone, lay in a shallow brook in North Carolina. As people passed, those who saw the stone never gave it a second look. One day a man who lived near by, while taking a walk, saw the stone and thought it might be useful as a doorstop for his cabin door, so took it home.

Sometime later, a geologist, passing through the area and not sure of his way, stopped at the cabin to ask for directions. The stone propped up against the cabin door caught his eye, for it was the largest lump of gold ever to be found east of the Rockies. The man who found the stone in the brook had seen no real value in it, but the geologist recognized its worth immediately.

Many who looked upon Jesus of Nazareth saw Him as simply a Galilean peasant. Others considered Him to be a great teacher or prophet. But some realized that He was the Eternal Son of God, and they yielded their lives to His control. When our Lord asked Peter, "Whom say ye that I am?" Peter confessed boldly, "Thou art the Christ, the Son of the living God" (Matthew 16:15-16).

Christ began and ended His earthly ministry as the Son of God, but this is not all. He has continued His ministry ever since as the Son of God, for "it is the Spirit that beareth witness, because the Spirit is truth." Everyone who believes on Christ for salvation receives the gift of the Holy Spirit, who enters the believer's life immediately to bear witness to "the truth." Our Lord had told His disciples of this: "And I will pray the

Father, and He shall give you another Comforter, that He may abide with you for ever" (John 14:16). How assuring it is to know that the Holy Spirit enters the believer's life at the time of his conversion, never to depart. From that moment on, "The Spirit [Himself] beareth witness with our spirit, that we are the children of God" (Romans 8:16).

Oftentimes the ministry of the Holy Spirit is hindered by a lack of our commitment to His control, for it is possible for one to be a possessor of the Holy Spirit while not being possessed by the Spirit. The believer who is possessed by the Holy Spirit will be an instrument in God's hands to be used to share the gospel with others.

Jesus Christ is the Son of God. This fact was depicted at Christ's baptism; it was depicted when He shed His blood on the cross; and it is depicted through the ministry of the Holy Spirit. Every Christian has the God-given responsibility of telling others about Christ. We tell them of the Divine Saviour through the divine agency of the Holy Spirit. God will give the wisdom, guidance, and the power to perform this task if only we will allow the Holy Spirit to have full control.

Paul wrote, "Redeeming the time, because the days are evil. Wherefore be ye not unwise, but understanding what the will of the Lord is. And be not drunk with wine, wherein is excess; but be filled with the Spirit" (Ephesians 5:16-18).

Three things listed here are imperative. First, God's people are to redeem the time because we are living in "days of evil." The only solution for the wickedness that abounds everywhere is salvation through Jesus Christ. It is obvious that Satan has influenced many in our churches to be satisfied with a "sit and listen"

Christianity rather than a "go ye" Christianity. Is it not true that most of our churches are merely inviting people to come, sit, and listen? More and more, the methodology seems to be one continuous series of meetings. This has been Satan's philosophy for centuries, substituting meetings for going. If we were asked to sum up what is being accomplished for God, we would have to put meetings at the top of the list. But if we expect to redeem the time in an evil and perverse generation, it will be necessary for us to break tradition. Instead of the "come and sit" philosophy we need a revolution, as urgently as in Luther's day, whereby Christians will be transformed from listeners to goers.

The second principle is that believers must not be "unwise," but "understanding what the will of the Lord is." Often the will of God is thought of as how it will benefit us personally. One will not always reap personal gain through doing God's will. In fact, in many cases just the opposite is true.

Primarily, the will of God concerns taking Christ to the lost. Without question, it is His will that the lost be saved and experience new life in Christ. "The Lord is not slack concerning His promise, as some men count slackness; but is longsuffering to usward, not willing that any should perish, but that all should come to repentance" (2 Peter 3:9). If God is "not willing that any should perish," neither should His people be willing. Priority for the will of God should not be to help ourselves, but to help others. We who are in Christ have received the light, but millions who are lost in their sins are living in darkness. For this reason, God says, "Be ye not unwise, but understanding what the will of the Lord is."

The third principle is that believers are commanded to be "filled with the Spirit." We are so to commit ourselves to the Holy Spirit's leadership that we shall be controlled by Him rather than by our weak, sinful flesh. When we are controlled by the flesh, we shall desire the things the flesh loves. When we are controlled by the Holy Spirit, we shall desire, above all else, to do God's will and communicate the gospel. When one is under the control of the Holy Spirit, he will lose sight of himself and his own interests in a sacrificial attempt to reach out of himself into the lives of those who need the Saviour.

It is appalling to consider the little concern to evangelize the lost that is obvious in the lives of many who profess to love Christ. On the other hand, have you noticed the fervor of some of these same believers in their quest to be successful and make money? God must be sorely grieved that they are more interested in business and money-making than in the souls of the lost.

I received a well-written letter from a large mail-order house, urging me to accept a free catalog as well as to sign an enclosed card to open a charge account. There was a self-addressed, stamped envelope to return the card. Not only that, a pencil was enclosed to make it convenient to sign. After reading the letter and examining the enclosures, I asked myself, "Am I as aggressive to get people to sign for Christ and eternity as these people are to get my business?" Are the people of the world willing to do more for money than we are for Christ?

Sometimes Christians say, "I know I should witness more, but I am afraid of offending people and driving them away." Never fear that you will offend or drive people away. You can drive them only in one direction— away from hell, for they are headed toward hell without Christ. How necessary it is that we pray daily that God will burden us to have an unresting compulsion to tell the unsaved about Jesus Christ.

In addition to the three witnesses in the earth there are three in Heaven: "For there are three that bear record in heaven, the Father, the Word, and the Holy Ghost: and these three are one." The authorities seem to agree that this verse does not belong in this Epistle. The oldest manuscripts do not contain these words. Possibly one of the scribes inserted them as a comment in the margin, and later, when copied by another, he assumed that they belonged in the text. We may be reasonably sure that verse 8 follows verse 6: "And there are three that bear witness in earth, the Spirit, and the water, and the blood: and these three agree in one." There is perfect harmony here because each of these witnesses depicts the same truth that Jesus Christ is the Son of God.

"If we receive the witness of men, the witness of God is greater: for this is the witness of God which He hath testified of His Son." All of us receive the witness of men, even though it is not always reliable. There have been times when we have discovered, much to our regret, that what we heard and believed proved to be untrue. If we are willing to believe humans who are prone to error, why should anyone doubt the infallible God? He, who cannot lie, sent His only Son into the world to die for our sins. When He was on this earth, Christ proved Himself to be the Son of God by healing the sick, giving sight to the blind, strengthening the brokenhearted, and raising the dead. Why should anyone disbelieve the Father's testimony about His Son?

"He that believeth on the Son of God hath the witness in himself." "The witness" is the Holy Spirit of verse 6, that comes to indwell the believer at conversion. The

Holy Spirit "is truth." Thus, though we cannot always believe what people tell us, we need never disbelieve God. The Holy Spirit within always speaks the truth.

It is an extremely serious matter to doubt God: "He that believeth not God hath made Him a liar; because he believeth not the record that God gave of His Son." Unbelief is far more serious than most of us realize, for it suggests that God is a deceiver. How foolish it is to doubt the Lord. We have reason to doubt humans, but God—never. All He has given us in His eternal Word is truth and it never needs revision. It is always up-to-date. All that God has spoken throughout the centuries concerning Himself and all of His works is as true today as when it was given. We are living in a changing world. Very little remains the same. Nations have changed; almost everything has been affected by change with one exception—God has not changed.

Someone has told of the earthquake that struck very suddenly in South America. In his description, he says the air was filled with clouds of dust, and the mountains were hurling their crags in the abysses. The birds were flying and screaming with terror. The wild beasts fled from their caves and ran abroad in fear. The very earth that seemed so solid was shaking beneath his feet like the ocean. But looking up to the sky he saw that it, alone was unchanged. It was calm, quiet and undisturbed.

The God who created the sky is still the same. His Holy Spirit is the same. His Son is the same. His Word is the same. Jesus Christ is "the same yesterday, and to day, and for ever" (Hebrews 13:8). God never changes. What He has recorded for us in the Scriptures will remain throughout eternity.

You have believed the witness of men, but have you believed the witness of God concerning His Son? John has told about the blind leaders of the blind in the religious world of his day. The same is true in our day. Many sincere people are being duped by false teachers who profess to have new light or new truth. Innocent victims are being deceived and being led into further darkness.

The late Dr. M. R. De Haan, in the devotional guide, *Our Daily Bread*, told of an elderly lady who stood hestitatingly at a corner as the traffic roared by. When the light changed, she continued to wait as she looked to the right and to the left to be sure all was clear. By the time she was ready, the light had changed again. She murmured to herself, "How I wish someone would help me across the street." Just then, an elderly gentleman approached and asked, "Will you permit me to walk across the intersection with you?" She readily answered, "Please!" He offered her his arm and they started across. About halfway, the man stumbled and almost fell. Impatiently, the lady said, "What's the matter with you? You walk as though you are blind!" To this came the astonishing reply, "Yes, I am blind. That's why I wanted to walk across the street with you."

There have been many sincere people who have sought for someone to give them spiritual guidance and help. Hearing the fanciful but appealing, unscriptural teachings of a false teacher, they readily responded to his shallow offer of an "easy way." To their dismay, however, they learned later that their so-called religious authority was nothing more than one of the many "blind leaders of the blind," sadly in need of help himself.

There is One, however, who can show us the true way because He is "the Way." The Lord Jesus Christ said, "I am the way, the truth, and the life: no man cometh unto the Father, but by Me" (John 14:6). God "hath in these last days spoken unto us by His Son" (Hebrews 1:2). There is no other Saviour but Christ. Believe the witness that God gave of His Son. Then allow the Holy Spirit to control your life that you might share this glorious truth with everyone you possibly can. Christ is alive, and He wants all men to be saved and prepared for eternity.

DURATION

And this is the record, that God hath given to us eternal life, and this life is in His Son. He that hath the Son hath life; and he that hath not the Son of God hath not life. These things have I written unto you that believe on the name of the Son of God; that ye may know that ye have eternal life, and that ye may believe on the name of the Son of God. And this is the confidence that we have in Him, that, if we ask any thing according to His will, He heareth us: And if we know that He hear us, whatsoever we ask, we know that we have the petitions that we desired of Him (1 John 5:11-15).

New life in Christ is not something granted on a loan basis. Through God's grace, it is given to the believer for a permanent possession. Though the child of God may not always live up to the standards set forth in the Scriptures, we can be certain that God will never fail His part of the transaction. His people may fail Him, but He will never fail His people. God's truth is established on verities that can neither be changed nor altered. God says, "Heaven and earth shall pass away, but My words shall not pass away" (Matthew 24:35).

How may one obtain eternal life? "And this is the record, that God hath given to us eternal life, and this life is in His Son." If one has truly received Christ, he need never wonder if he is saved. It will not be necessary for him to wait until he dies to get the answer. He may know immediately, the very moment he trusts in Christ. If ever he is prone to doubt, he should go to this verse in 1 John and read carefully, "that God *hath given* to us eternal life."

Of course, if one attempts to meet the Lord any other way than through Christ, it is understandable why he might doubt. If he had simply an emotional experience without a real heart belief in the Lord, he will not receive new life in Christ, for we are told that "this life is in His Son." One does not receive "this life" by joining a church, baptism, attempting to keep the commandments, doing the best he can, or any other way. It is only by receiving Jesus Christ as Saviour and Lord.

The Scriptures make it very clear that when anyone receives Christ, he is saved for all eternity. In his Gospel, John records the words of our Lord that substantiate this truth: "My sheep hear My voice, and I know them, and they follow Me: and I give unto them eternal life; and they shall never perish, neither shall any man pluck them out of My hand. My Father, which gave them Me, is greater than all; and no man is able to pluck them out of My Father's hand" (John 10:27-29).

An attractive lady came forward in one of my meetings to receive Christ. In counseling her, following the service, I learned that she was deeply convicted because of the sinful life she had been living since the death of her husband. The sin of adultery had given her a guilt complex that allowed no rest. As we prayed, she confessed her wrongdoing to the Lord. She then asked if I thought there was any hope for her. It was my pleasure to point her to God's truth as recorded in John 1:12, "But as many as received Him, to them gave He power to become the [children] of God, even to them that believe on His name." I explained that receiving Christ always results in new life and the forgiveness of all our sins. She readily believed and grasped the truth of God as a drowning person reaches for any available help. God met this believer in a marvelous way. Her life was transformed by the power of God and she became a new creature in Christ. A life that was being wasted in sin suddenly became one that has since been used mightily for God.

What actually happened to this guilt-ridden, miserable, unhappy person that revolutionized her entire life? Did she vow to do better? Was it simply new resolves with a willing heart? It was far more; she became the recipient of eternal life through the Son of God. This same experience is for all who are willing to recognize their sinfulness before the Lord and receive Jesus Christ.

But how can one be sure that belief in Christ is the right way? There are many religions in the world that offer various ways of escape from sin. But only Christianity offers the one way that has stood the test of time. "The faith which was once delivered unto the saints" is filled with certainties. God has given a "record," not only through John's writings, but in all of Scripture in which He speaks repeatedly in precept and type as He presents the great truth of eternal life through His Son, Jesus Christ. The religions of the world are established on the weak and flimsy foundation of what men have taught and said. The Christian faith is substantiated by what God has said.

Surely, for any honest searcher of truth, nothing could be clearer than "he that hath the Son hath life; and he that hath not the Son of God hath not life." The "life" spoken of here is eternal life. Do you have eternal life? Don't say, "I think so." The Word of God makes it plain that either you have eternal life or you do not have it. If you only "think" you have eternal life, you are failing to believe God's Word. Maybe your reply to the question is, "I hope so." That isn't sufficient, either. If you have believed on the Son, then you have eternal life. If you have not trusted in Christ, there is no need to speculate, for you do not have eternal life.

A Christian young man was on a mountain-climbing trip with some friends. During an extremely heavy downpour of rain the men decided to remain in their tent. They talked about various things and ultimately got on the subject of religion. One of the young men, a scientist, turned to the known Christian, and with an air of superiority, said, "You don't really believe that Jesus is the Son of God, do you?" "I certainly do," replied the Christian. "But how can you prove it? How do you know this is true?" The Christian looked the man in the eye and said, "I know Jesus Christ is the Son of God because I know Him personally." Nothing more was said. Argument would have been useless. Every true Christian knows Jesus Christ personally, and with such a relationship, there need be no doubt about eternal life.

One of the reasons John wrote his first Epistle was to help believers realize that in Christ they may know that they possess eternal life. "These things have I written unto you that believe on the name of the Son of God; that ye may know that ye have eternal life, and that ye may believe on the name of the Son of God." The apostle was not concerned only that the unsaved believe on Christ and be saved; he wanted them to know they were saved after they believed.

Many believers lack the assurance of their salvation. Oftentimes this lack is due to a failure on the part of other believers to adequately instruct and follow-up the new converts. It is extremely important after one is saved that he faithfully study the Scriptures so he "*may know*" he is saved.

One who has sincerely received Christ into his life, need never doubt his salvation. The Bible assures us that we "are kept by the power of God" (1 Peter 1:5), and that God "hath begotten us again unto a lively hope" (1 Peter 1:3). The "lively hope" is God's gift so that we may know we have eternal life.

It seems that the word "know" is one of John's favorites. He uses it no less than 177 times in his writings. He was not one to dwell on uncertainty. He dealt with facts. We need to do the same. No one gets very far if he doesn't know where he is going. Effort is best sustained by certainty. This is true of salvation. We should not doubt, but take God at His word. We are not to wonder about our salvation, but believe and thank God for it. Martin Luther was asked one time if he "felt" that his sins were forgiven. "No," he replied. "I don't feel that they are forgiven. I *know they are* because God says so in His Word."

Regardless of what God has said in His Word, there are some who feel that they must help God. They talk about their good life, or what they do, rather than what Jesus Christ has done. Christ is the One who died for our sins and through His death, as the humble servant of God, condescended to our level: "He humbled Himself, and became obedient unto death, even the death of the cross" (Philippians 2:8). In His selfless sacrifice, Christ was made "to be sin for us, who knew no sin; that we might be made the righteousness of God in Him" (2 Corinthians 5:21). Indeed, He earned well the right to be the Saviour of all. No human ever earned this right. The best of us is sinful and in need of Christ's redemption. God made possible the great provision of eternal life so that those who believe might "know" that they are saved. Thus we see from God's Word that nothing, other than the sacrifice of Christ, is sufficient for salvation. If anyone is to be saved, there is only one way: we must come to God through Christ, and receive salvation as a free gift.

A Sunday school teacher, wishing to impress his class with the truth that salvation must be received as a gift, took his expensive watch off his wrist and offered it to one of the boys in his class. "It's yours if you'll take it," he said. The boy sat grinning, thinking his teacher was joking. The teacher turned and offered the watch to another boy, saying the same words. The little fellow smiled, also. Feeling he would be laughed at if he held out his hand, like the first boy, he did nothing. Finally, after getting the same response from each one in the class, the teacher turned to the last boy. When the watch was offered to him, he reached out and took it, while the rest of the class exchanged humorous glances. The teacher said, "I am thankful you believed my word, son. The watch is yours to keep." The rest of the class looked in amazement. There was much talk when the class was over. The boys could be heard saying, "I wish I had known that; I would have taken it."

As that teacher offered the boys the expensive watch, so God offers everyone His priceless salvation which cannot in any way be compared with all the money in the world. "What shall it profit a man, if he shall gain the whole world, and lose his own soul? Or what shall a man give in exchange for his soul?" (Mark 8:36-37) It is not by what we do that saves us, but by what Christ has done. Those who believe on Him become the possessors of eternal life, and for this reason, they should "know" that they are saved.

"And this is the confidence that we have in Him, that, if we ask anything according to His will, He heareth us: And if we know that He hear us, whatsoever we ask, we know that we have the petitions that we desired of Him." The word "confidence," used here, means *boldness*. It is understandable that a person, considering God's superiority as the Creator of the universe, might shy away from the privilege of prayer, thinking, "Who am I, poor, puny me, that I can call on the eternal God!" But we don't call on God in our name; it is Christ's name that makes possible the efficacy of prayer. That's why all prayer should be addressed to God "in Christ's name." Since prayer power is realized on the basis of our relationship to the Son of God, the sincere believer can approach God with "boldness." We are instructed to "come boldly unto the throne of grace, that we may obtain mercy, and find grace to help in time of need" (Hebrews 4:16). What a privilege is ours in Christ! We need not fear to ask for the "great and mighty things" that God has promised.

After his release, Robert Vogeler was asked many times how he was able to get through seventeen months of solitary confinement in a communist prison without cracking up mentally and physically. He said that "it was only possible because of the power of prayer. The thing the communists forgot, or perhaps they did not know, was that no matter how deep the dungeon or how thick its walls, or how heavily guarded, they could not keep Almighty God out of the prisoner's mind and heart. Nor could they keep the praise of God from one's lips." It was the realization of this soul-stirring knowledge that brought Robert Vogeler through the horrors imposed upon Him by the communists. Though a captive and subdued by men, with boldness he could go to God in prayer to find that His grace was sufficient.

For the believer, prayer should be the key to the day and the lock to the night. It should not be a convenience to use only in emergencies, but a privilege to enjoy, moment by moment. Paul wrote, "Pray without ceasing" (1 Thessalonians 5:17). We are to keep in touch with God constantly. All things are to be done with full dependence upon His wisdom and help.

We need only to read God's Word to see what prayer has done. "It has divided seas, rolled up the flowing rivers, made flinty rocks gush into fountains, quenched flames of fire, muzzled lions, disarmed vipers, burst open iron gates, recalled souls from eternity, conquered the strongest devils, and commanded legions of angels down from Heaven." Why should any of us need to be exhorted to pray, when we recognize from God's truth the mighty miracles that have been wrought through prayer?

God hears our prayers when "we ask any thing according to His will." This is not to suggest that before we call on the Lord we must determine carefully if what we are asking coincides with the will of God. We are to do the praying, and God will do the sorting. Of course, we are not to ask for anything that is unscriptural or sinful. But if one is growing in grace and seeking to follow the Lord in a life of obedience, he should have no fear of unloading the burdens of his heart at any time on the shoulders of the Almighty. When he does, if what he is requesting is in accordance with God's will, the believer may be assured of God's response.

"He heareth us" should not be understood to mean that *He granteth us.* God is not restricted to answer our prayers as we pray them. He promises only to hear us. He will answer according to His will. People have been heard to say that God did not answer their prayers, intimating that God did not hear them. What they should have said was that God did not answer their prayers as they prayed them. God always answers prayer. But our petitions are altered by His will. We can be thankful for this, for if God were to provide answers apart from His will, the consequences could be disastrous. It should be kept in mind that one of the important requisites for effectual prayer is the will of God. If the Lord Jesus prayed, "Not My will, but Thine, be done" (Luke 22:42), how much more important it is for all believers to pray in the same manner, for prayers answered in the will of God will always be for God's glory and our good.

If one is not walking with the Lord, in close fellowship with Him, seeking to please Him in every area of his life, his prayers will usually be selfish, and as the result, ineffectual. James reminds us that "the effectual fervent prayer of a righteous man availeth much" (James 5:16). A righteous man is one who is allowing God to live through him and control his life. Prayer is more than asking God for things; it is fellowship and communion with Him. If one is not enjoying this kind of harmonious relationship with the Lord, probably he will be like those of whom James writes, saying, "Ye ask, and receive not, because ye ask amiss, that ye may consume it upon your lusts" (James 4:3). What James is describing is a misconception of what true prayer should be. Prayer fellowship with the Almighty is wonderful fellowship, and because of it God performs mighty miracles.

A casual reading of verse 15 might look as though God gives us everything we ask for: "And if we know that He hear us, whatsoever we ask, we know that we have the petitions that we desired of Him." The important part of this verse is not "Whatsoever we ask," but rather, "if we know that He hear us." Considering the previous verse, what petitions does God hear? "Any thing according to His will." Petitions that are in the will of God will be heard and answered according to His will. Thus we have another of John's certainties: "we know" that God will answer our prayers in a manner pleasing to Him. This is a marvelous assurance.

Most of us can think back over the years of our lives and recall some of the things for which we prayed and did not receive. Now we can praise God that we did not get them for we found that God had a better plan. At the time, we were disappointed, but now we know better. On the other hand, there were some things for which we prayed and did not get, which we cannot understand. But God does, and that is all that matters. One thing is certain; even though we cannot understand, the perfect will of God was fulfilled and there is no improvement upon that. For this reason we need never question anything which enters the life of the believer. As we pray, God's will is being experienced. Though it may mean pain and suffering, and sometimes even heartbreak, we have the assurance of knowing that "we have the petitions that we desired of Him." The disposition of our prayers rests in the wise counsel of Almighty God, who makes no mistakes and gives only His best to those who love Him. Thomas a Kempis expressed this well as he said, "Give what Thou wilt, and how much

Thou wilt, and when Thou wilt. See me where Thou wilt, and deal with me in all things as Thou wilt." When one calls on the Lord with such an attitude of submission to God's wisdom and direction, he will experience the joy of believing prayer.

George Muller offers a splendid example of God's faithfulness in this kind of praying. This dedicated servant of Christ was heard to say, "During my lifetime, I have had 25,000 prayers answered and 5,000 of these came on the very day I made the petition." Muller kept a ledger for his prayer requests in which was a double entry. On one side was the nature of the request and the date which waited to be matched on the other side by the answer and the date on which it came. Checking through this record, this man of God, who read the Bible through two hundred times, found that the Lord specifically changed his prayers into realities.

Muller was accused of having a secret stairway into Heaven because of his many answers to prayer. He answered his critics: "I've had a policy in my life that when I read the Word of God and come to a commandment, I obey it immediately." No wonder Muller experienced the mighty workings of God. But realize that what Muller enjoyed through prayer was not for him only: it is for all of us who know Christ. As we claim Him as Lord of all and seek to do His will, prayer will be more than a duty: it will be a blessed privilege.

DISTRACTION

If any man see his brother sin a sin which is not unto death, he shall ask, and he shall give him life for them that sin not unto death. There is a sin unto death: I do not say that he shall pray for it. All unrighteousness is sin: and there is a sin not unto death. We know that whosoever is born of God sinneth not; but he that is begotten of God keepeth himself, and that wicked one toucheth him not. And we know that we are of God, and the whole world lieth in wickedness. And we know that the Son of God is come, and hath given us an understanding, that we may know Him that is true, and we are in Him that is true, even in His Son Jesus Christ. This is the true God, and eternal life. Little children, keep yourselves from idols. Amen (1 John 5:16-21).

The apostle concludes his short Epistle on the same note which he began. In the opening chapter, he stressed the importance of the believer's walking "in the light," as opposed to walking "in darkness." In his conclusion, he emphasizes this same thought as he warns of sin's power.

Sin is always a hindrance to God's blessing. It is the distraction Satan uses to turn believers from the Lord's best. As followers of Christ, we need to be ever mindful and watchful of the subtle attacks of our enemy, designed to destroy Christian victory. Satan hates the believer as he hates God, and does all he can to destroy our witness.

Christians are obligated, not only for their own relationship to the Lord, but for that of their brothers and
sisters in Christ. We are told that "none of us liveth to
himself, and no man dieth to himself" (Romans 14:7).
In a very special sense, those who are in the family of
God belong to each other. The problems other Christians
face are in reality our problems too. With love we should
share with them in their conflicts. God says, "Bear ye
one another's burdens, and so fulfil the law of Christ"
(Galatians 6:2). There should be no such person as a
"loner" among God's people. With a holy concern for
each other, we are to "rejoice with them that do rejoice,
and weep with them that weep" (Romans 12:15).

We have a personal responsibility for other Christians.
"If any man see his brother sin a sin which is not unto
death, he shall ask, and [God] shall give him life for
them that sin not unto death." In caring for the spiritual
needs of our brothers and sisters in Christ who have
yielded to temptation, we are not to respond with a
critical spirit. Rather, with hearts overflowing with love,
we should help in every way possible to get them back
in fellowship with the Lord. The Lord has forgiven each
of us many, many times and restored us to fellowship.
Because of this, we are obligated to help fellow believers
in their times of defeat so they might once again "press
toward the mark for the prize of the high calling of God
in Christ Jesus" (Philippians 3:14).

As we help other Christians through their encounters
with Satan, we ourselves will become stronger in the
Lord. As the result, we shall be better prepared to face
the wicked one. We lose nothing when we reach out in
love to a fallen brother or sister; we gain everything.
This obviously is what is meant by Paul's admonition:
"Brethren, if a man be overtaken in a fault, ye which are

spiritual, restore such an one in the spirit of meekness; considering thyself, lest thou also be tempted" (Galatians 6:1).

There are several ways we can help believers who are facing spiritual problems. One of the most important is prayer: "If any man see his brother sin a sin which is not unto death, he shall ask." Before we do anything else, we are to pray. Very little can be accomplished, when dealing with sin, without much prayer. Before saying anything to another about his spiritual need, we must spend adequate time with God to prepare our own hearts. When the emphasis on private prayer is overlooked, usually our best efforts will prove fruitless.

One of the noticeable lessons presented in the book of Acts is that prayer is not simply for emergencies. It is God's routine method of getting things done.

Few of us have the burden we should for prayer. It is worth while that we pray daily for our friends and loved ones, and others who come to mind, that God will keep them from temptation and sin. If we know of those who are struggling with evil, we should agonize at the mercy seat for them. John Wesley once said, "God does nothing but in answer to prayer." The reason why God's people fail so frequently in their walk with the Lord must be a lack of prayer. We need to get serious about the ministry of prayer if we expect to defeat the devil.

James wrote, "Confess your faults one to another, and pray one for another, that ye may be healed. The effectual fervent prayer of a righteous man availeth much" (James 5:16). It is evident from this verse that prayer is essential for physical healing. But in the previous verse, you will see that the sickness spoken of here is the result of known sin in the believer's life:

"[Since] *he [has] committed sins*, they shall be forgiven him." Here again we see that prayer is imperative. It is requisite that we be compassionately concerned for our Christian brothers and sisters, and intercede for them in the midst of their spiritual struggles.

There is one exception to the rule. Prayer is in order under all circumstances but one: "There is a sin unto death: I do not say that he shall pray for it." Some have suggested that this might refer to the unpardonable sin such as the blasphemy of the Holy Spirit. Others feel that it is the sin of apostasy, of which John writes in this Epistle. But since the article does not appear before "sin" in the original, the verse is not referring to one particular sin but to any one of many. In my thinking, it would seem to be habitual disobedience and rebellion to God by continuing in known sin after one's conversion. God says, "Therefore to him that knoweth to do good, and doeth it not, to him it is sin" (James 4:17). Consequently, if a believer persists in committing a particular sin with the knowledge that it is wrong, God may choose to chasten him in the body with sickness, and in some cases physical death. The use of "death" in verse 16 means physical death, not spiritual.

Though not all sickness and physical death are the result of persisting in sin, often they are. Several notable examples are given in the Scriptures, such as Ananias and Sapphira who lied to the Holy Spirit; the professed believers at Corinth who abused the Lord's table; and Moses and Aaron who smote the rock because of their anger. God saw fit to judge these and other Biblical characters physically as He does with believers in our day who continue to walk in darkness.

It is a serious matter to live on such a low plain as to desecrate the grace of God. Under such circumstances there is no need to pray for such a person, for this is a matter between the believer and God only. Until he comes to the Lord voluntarily, and confesses and forsakes his sin, our prayers will be of no avail. The disobedient believer is openly resisting the mercy of God, and bringing judgment upon himself by his continual defiance.

Of course, sympathetic Christians are not always knowledgeable to the extent that they can discern whether one is really committing "sin unto death." No harm is done if prayer is offered for the erring one; it is just that the prayers will not be effectual if there is "sin unto death."

So there might not be any misunderstanding, we are told what sin is: "All unrighteousness is sin: and there is a sin not unto death." What is not right is wrong. How does one know what is not right? Who is the judge? Certainly sinful humans do not have this prerogative. We are no better than those who lived during the time of the judges when "every man did that which was right in his own eyes" (Judges 21:25). This same philosophy is evident in our present day, and as the result the world is in a mess.

"Right" has to do with righteousness. This doesn't leave much hope for humans, for the Bible tells us "there is none righteous, no, not one" (Romans 3:10). This rules man out and leaves only God to set the standard. Of Him, we read in Psalm 11:7, "For the righteous LORD loveth righteousness." Because God is righteous, He is the One who determines right or wrong.

In His written Word, the Bible, the Holy Spirit has revealed the way of righteousness through Jesus Christ, the living Word. After one enters into a personal relationship with the Son, he is obligated to please Him in everything as he obeys the teachings of the written Word. Failure to obey the Word is unrighteousness, and "unrighteousness is sin."

The most expensive thing in all the world is sin. Many have been deceived by it through a glass of sparkling liquid. The pleasure passed quickly, and the thoughtless drinker became the trapped alcoholic. Sometimes, sin appears in the form of a needle. It seems harmless until the brain is damaged and the life is ruined. It comes casually, as a suggestion to a young girl. Beguiled by the thought of "try and see," purity is smeared by lust. It enters homes. What might have been a happy home is badgered by nagging, unfaithfulness, and ultimately divorce, while little children suffer the destructive effects of sin. It approaches the man in business, suggesting "shortcuts" to success. Cheating becomes a way of life, while the good name disappears and the business strikes the downgrade. Even our churches are not immune. The harmony of the saints can soon become disharmony as the will of man supplants the will of God.

Oh, believer in Christ, consider the awfulness of sin. Recognize it as the reason for which Christ died. It was our sin that nailed Him to the cross. We who have been redeemed from sin, must forsake all sin, if we are to please our heavenly Father. The task is not beyond us, for this is why Christ came. The message of the angel to Joseph is God's message to all true believers, "And she shall bring forth a son, and thou shalt call His name JESUS: for *He shall save His people from their sins*" (Matthew 1:21). We are enabled by Christ's life within to claim victory over our sin. If we resist the Lord in this, we are no better than before we were converted. God saved us to be a different kind of people, new creations through whom He can work.

"We know that whosoever is born of God sinneth not; but he that is begotten of God keepeth himself, and that wicked one toucheth him not." This does not mean that after one is saved he cannot sin. It is that after one is saved, he should not continue to practice sin. As the result of his spiritual rebirth, he should live as a citizen of Heaven, even though presently he is dwelling in the midst of the darkness of this earth. "We are [God's] workmanship, created in Christ Jesus unto good works, which God hath before ordained that we should walk in them" (Ephesians 2:10). Good works are in contrast to evil works. The child of God should evidence his new life by a holy walk, "for God hath not called us unto uncleanness, but unto holiness" (1 Thessalonians 4:7).

Because one is a Christian is no promise that sin will not continue to be a problem. Our sinful nature has not been eradicated. But the beauty of it is that in Christ we have received a new nature. No longer must we be dominated by the old, for we can live in the strength and power of the new. There will be times when the old nature will be in control, and the believer will yield to sin. But as he confesses to the Lord with a desire to obey, God forgives him immediately. The sin that was committed is "sin not unto death." It is under the blood forever, and again the believer is in fellowship with the Lord. But one may confess his sin and habitually repeat the same sin while failing to claim God's power to overcome it. For this there is no forgiveness until there is sincere repentance. This is "sin unto death," resulting in God's chastening.

It is abnormal for true children of God to continue in sin after coming to the Lord: "We know that whosoever is born of God sinneth not; but he that is begotten of God keepeth himself, and that wicked one toucheth him not." As before, "sinneth not" is not a suggestion of sinless perfection. If one is truly "born of God," he does not continue in the practice of sin. He forsakes the ways of sin and desires, above all else, to please the Lord and follow Him. Though he is still a sinner by nature, he is a redeemed sinner with new ambitions and motives.

It is obvious from the latter part of verse 18 that the Christian is in continuous conflict with Satan: "He that is begotten of God keepeth himself, and that wicked one toucheth him not." To keep one's self does not mean that we are to resist Satan in our own strength. All of us, in ourselves, are too weak for that. There are scores of Scripture verses that tell us the believer's responsibility is to lean on the Lord completely and allow Him to fight the battle for us. As we trust Christ for His power, the devil cannot touch us.

Because of God's marvelous provision, there is never a time when the child of God need be defeated by sin. The Lord Jesus declared, "All power is given unto Me in heaven and in earth" (Matthew 28:18). This is not "some" power, or "limited" power. It is *all* power. Through Jesus Christ, the believer has sufficient power to overcome any temptation the deceiver might thrust before him.

Satan is mighty, but Christ our redeemer is almighty: "We know that we are of God, and the whole world lieth in wickedness." As used here, "wickedness" could be translated *the wicked one*. Satan is the "god of this world" (2 Corinthians 4:4). He is the one who controls the present world system that opposes God and righteousness. He is also the god and father of all who have not yet confessed Jesus as Saviour and Lord. There are two classes of humanity: those who are children of God and those who are children of the devil. These are the two opposite and opposing forces living in the present world. This will continue until Christ returns, at which time everyone will bow to Christ and confess that He is Lord. Satan will be bound for a thousand years, and Christ will reign in righteousness. But until Christ returns, Satan will continue as the powerful enemy of all that is right and good.

How assuring it is for the child of God to know that we never need face this disrupter of peace and blessing in our own strength. The all-conquering and all-powerful Christ is ready and willing to give us all the strength and power we need to live victoriously.

Every believer possesses the potentiality for good or evil. Since he has both an old and new nature, he can be a tool for evil or a vessel for good. In himself, the believer is not sufficient to make the proper choices: "With men, this is impossible; but with God all things are possible" (Matthew 19:26). As Paul has shown us, there must be complete yieldedness to Christ: "I can do all things through Christ which strengtheneth me" (Philippians 4:13). Yielded to Christ, the believer is a conquering power for good: "We are of God." What blessing we enjoy as we live in joyful obedience to our Lord, forsaking all sin to follow Him.

"*We know* that whosoever is born of God sinneth not." "*We know* that we are of God." "*We know* that the Son of God is come, and hath given us an understanding, that we may *know* Him that is true, and we are in Him that is true, even in His Son Jesus Christ. This is the true God, and eternal life." It is possible for everyone to know Jesus Christ, who is both "God, and eternal life." Do you know Him? Have you definitely asked Him to come into your life as Saviour and Lord? If not, do not delay. God loves you and He wants you to enjoy His best.

The Epistle concludes with a warning for believers: "Little children, keep yourselves from idols." How needful it is that those of us who have been born into the family of God be ever watchful of any idols that might distract our attention from the One and True God. Usually an idol is thought of as a statue of some kind. Actually an idol is any object of preference which makes God fall behind it. The list of things that could be preferred before God is endless. It could be a person, a car, sports, television, antiques, a home, children, lust, and many more.

A believer can be an idol worshiper and not realize it. He might wonder why he is so limited and ineffective for God. It could be idol worship. When our Lord was asked, "Which is the great commandment in the law?" His reply was, "Thou shalt love the Lord thy God with all thy heart, and with all thy soul, and with all thy mind. This is the first and great commandment" (Matthew 22:36-38). This is still "the first and great commandment."

Do you love Jesus Christ with all your heart, and with all your soul, and with all your mind? If so, then you know the blessedness of *living confidently*. One of these days you will be with your living, loving Lord to praise Him throughout eternity, along with the great host of saints who have been redeemed by the blood of the Lamb.

THE SECOND EPISTLE

OF JOHN

2 JOHN

APPRECIATION

The elder unto the elect lady and her children, whom I love in the truth; and not I only, but also all they that have known the truth; For the truth's sake, which dwelleth in us, and shall be with us for ever. Grace be with you, mercy, and peace, from God the Father, and from the Lord Jesus Christ, the Son of the Father, in truth and love (2 John 1-3).

Though an apostle, John writes as "the elder," which suggests that he had been entrusted with leadership responsibility over a large area of churches. He was the "general pastor" to whom the local pastors and their people could go for counseling and help. John, like Paul, never gloried in his divine call as an apostle, but humbly offered himself for any service that was needed in the body of Christ.

The Epistle is addressed to "the elect lady and her children." Some have considered "the elect lady" to be a reference to the Church as a whole or a particular assembly of believers. Without question, what is taught in the Epistle is for the Church, but the elect lady seems to be a certain faithful Christian woman who was well known for her fidelity to the truth. The greetings expressed in verse 13 from her sister's children strongly suggest that the elect lady was an individual.

The elect lady was highly respected and loved by the Lord's people. John expressed his heart-felt appreciation for her: "Whom I love in the truth and not I only, but also all they that have known the truth." The love expressed here has to do with the wonderful bond of fellowship that exists between dedicated saints, which is rarely effected by selfish whims or imaginations. It prayerfully overlooks the failures of others while abstaining from criticism and petty unkindness.

This is the love described so beautifully in 1 Corinthians 13:4-7 that "suffereth long, and is kind," that "envieth not," that "vaunteth not itself," nor is it "puffed up." It "doth not behave itself unseemly," it "seeketh not her own," it "is not easily provoked, thinketh no evil," it "rejoiceth not in iniquity, but rejoiceth in the truth." It "beareth all things, believeth all things, hopeth all things, endureth all things."

A young Christian couple lived with the husband's unsaved father. It seemed that no matter how hard the wife tried to please her father-in-law, everything she did was criticized by him. Not only was he extremely critical, but very abusive and profane. Greatly disturbed and becoming more and more frustrated, the young wife sought the advice of her pastor.

After listening to her story, the pastor asked, "Is there anything special your father-in-law likes to eat?"

"Yes," she replied, "chocolate fudge."

"Then," said the pastor, "every time he is unkind to you, make him some chocolate fudge."

One day he requested some hot coffee with the added comment, "and I mean hot!" As it was handed to him, the cup slipped and the hot coffee showered his leg, provoking a string of curse words such as the young wife had never heard before. At first she was tempted to retaliate, but God gave her grace to return to the kitchen without a word. Suddenly her thoughts went to chocolate fudge. She mixed the ingredients quickly and soon it was ready to serve. She brought it to the angry father-in-law who turned his head and refused to touch it. After several kindly appeals, he gave in. As he tasted it, there was quiet. Then the daughter-in-law noticed a tear on his cheek. While staring at the dish of fudge, he said slowly, "I want to know the God who made you do this for me."

Love never fails. John knew this very well. He had experienced God's love through Christ and manifested it in his life. Furthermore, as the result of John's testimony, God's love was evidenced in the lives of many in the churches under his supervision. These people had received "the truth," and when one apprehends "the truth," the love of God is shed abroad in his heart by the Holy Ghost (Romans 5:5). As the believer permits the Holy Spirit to control his life, love for others will be the result.

John greets the elect lady with "grace, mercy, and peace." Grace is a reminder of Christ's sacrifice on the cross. Mercy has to do with the forgiveness of sin made possible by the blood shed on the cross. Peace means "to bind," establishing an indissoluble relationship between the repentant believer and the eternal God. This relationship results in a quietness and assurance of soul that can be known in no other way. How marvelous it is to experience God's grace, mercy, and peace, as revealed in the person of our "Lord Jesus Christ, the Son of the Father, in truth and love."

GRATIFICATION

I rejoiced greatly that I found of thy children walking in
truth, as we have received a commandment from the Father
(2 John 4).

The elect lady was known not only for her dedication
to the Lord, but also for her devotion to her family. Her
busy activity for God never interfered with her moral
responsibility as a mother to rear her children to follow
the Lord. John was quick to commend her for this.
Surely there is no work for God more necessary than for
a mother to do her best to lead her children in the way
of the Lord.

John "rejoiced greatly" for what he had seen in the
lives of the children of the elect lady. Doubtless he had
been disappointed on occasion by what he had seen in
the children of some of the other believers. But as he
traveled about in the cause of his ministry, it was a
gratifying experience to fellowship with the children
of the elect lady and to find them "walking in truth."

It is not enough to know the truth, or to even believe
the truth. God's people are obligated to be "walking in
truth." It is hardly to be expected of one who really
knows and believes the truth that he would do anything
other than walk in truth. John must have had this in

mind when he wrote 1 John 2:6, "He that saith he abideth in Him ought himself also so to walk, even as [Christ] walked." Without question, a person's manner of life provides the evidence of his relationship to the Lord. If one continues to live contrary to the teachings of Scripture, is it possible that he has met the Lord? It is certainly questionable.

The Christian walk is not optional. If one has truly believed in Christ, it is imperative that he live for the Lord, for "we have received a commandment from the Father." Repeatedly God commands us in the Word to walk so as to honor His name. In Romans 6:4 we are told "that like as Christ was raised up from the dead by the glory of the Father, even so we also should walk in newness of life." Paul wrote to the Ephesian saints, "See then that ye walk circumspectly, not as fools, but as wise, redeeming the time, because the days are evil" (Ephesians 5:15-16). To the Colossians he wrote, "As ye have therefore received Christ Jesus the Lord, so walk ye in Him" (Colossians 2:6). By our walk we prove our faith and make our "calling and election sure" (2 Peter 1:10).

An aged missionary, while fulfilling his labors in Argentina, was stricken suddenly with appendicitis. Because of the delay caused by several days of travel to the needed surgeon, the outlook for the operation was not too favorable.

After a careful examination of the patient, the surgeon said, "We must operate immediately, but with your age and the delay there is only one chance in a hundred for recovery." The surgeon then asked, "Have you ever used alcoholic liquors? Have you ever used tobacco in any form?" The missionary replied that he had never used either.

The operation was performed and proved to be a success. The blood of the patient was so pure that the wound healed like the flesh of a child. Later the surgeon said to the missionary, "You are a walking temperance lesson."

Not only should any believer be "a walking temperance lesson," but his Christian walk should be such that everyone who observes him will know that he belongs to God. Too few believers seem to be living in a way that the unsaved are drawn to Christ because of their convincing walk with the Lord.

Some months ago, Dr. David E. Smith, a prominent Christian ophthalmologist in our city was drowned while vacationing with his family. Being a patient of Dr. Smith's, and in need of eye surgery several months later, I was informed by the clinic that Dr. Julian C. Culton was caring for some of Dr. Smith's patients.

While being examined by Dr. Culton, I said, "I suppose you miss Dr. Smith around here."

"Yes, we do," was his reply. "In fact," he continued, "I have a special affinity for Dr. Smith because he led me to Christ."

Upon further questioning, I was told by Dr. Culton that having sensed a need in his own life, he initiated a visit with Dr. Smith to discuss spiritual matters. I asked why he especially chose to see Dr. Smith rather than someone else. Without hesitation he made it clear to me that it was the life Dr. Smith had lived. He was kind and gracious without any evidence of hostility at any time. His character was irreproachable.

Dr. Smith was the epitome of those John wrote about who were "walking in truth, as we have received a commandment from the Father." Indeed, this should be the experience for every child of God. We cannot afford to do anything less than to "walk in the light, as [Christ] is in the light" (1 John 1:7).

EXHORTATION

And now I beseech thee, lady, not as though I wrote a new commandment unto thee, but that which we had from the beginning, that we love one another. And this is love, that we walk after His commanments. This is the commandment, That, as ye have heard from the beginning, ye should walk in it." (2 John 5-6).

John could not stay away from the theme of love. Since the day he experienced God's love in conversion, it was so much a part of him that he spoke and wrote of it constantly. As in his other writings, we find him reverting to it again in the verses before us.

The love John wrote about was not a passion or emotion, but a life principle. It is God's loving life controlling the believer. The greater one's commitment to the Lord's control, the more evident this love will be.

With strong appeal, John implores the elect lady to manifest God's love: "I beseech thee, lady . . . that we love one another." Realizing the constant need of his own heart, John was careful to include himself in this entreaty.

One may be versatile in many ways as he exercises his God-given abilities. But without the free flow of

God's love through his life, all his efforts will be "as sounding brass, or a tinkling cymbal" (1 Corinthians 13:1).

What John wrote about love was not new. In fact, it was as old as God Himself, "for God is love" (1 John 4:8). In this sense, love is "from the beginning." As the result, every relationship in the believer's life from conversion to glory, should be a manifestation of God's love. Since "God so loved us, we ought also to love one another (1 John 4:11).

The gift of God's love to the believer is not merely for enjoyment; it obligates us to obey the Word of the Lord. "This is love, that we walk after His commandments." It is not enough to talk about God's love; we must reveal it in our lives.

A husband could tell his wife a dozen times a day that he loves her, but unless he proves it with kindness and faithfulness, his words would be meaningless.

So it is with the Christian. It is not enough to tell of our love for the Lord. Because God's love is a life principle, we are expected to live it out, or as John says, "Ye should walk in it." When we walk in it we shall "love one another" under all circumstances.

At no time should the believer act in any way other than by love. If he does, it is obvious that he is controlled by the flesh. It is God's desire that His love flow through the believer constantly.

The King James Version states John's commandment to love as "that which *we had* from the beginning." But the original reads "that which *we have* from the beginning." Love is always the believer's *present* obligation. To fail to love everyone at all times is to live in disobedience. For "this is the commandment" that "ye have heard from the beginning." God's commandments are not given to be believed; they are to be obeyed. He commands "that we love one another."

At no time will the Lord accept anything in lieu of obedience. The fact that one teaches Sunday school or even preaches is of little value if he has enmity in his heart. God says that he is to love; if he does not love his neighbor as himself his service is ineffectual for he is living in disobedience.

King Saul had a heart filled with hatred for David. He thought he could hide his sin by offering sacrifices to God. But ultimately the Lord judged Saul for his defiance. God declared through His servant Samuel, "Hath the LORD as great delight in burnt offerings and sacrifices, as in obeying the voice of the LORD? Behold, to obey is better than sacrifice, and to hearken than the fat of rams" (1 Samuel 15:22).

A famous children's specialist once said, "When it comes to a serious illness, the child who has been taught to obey stands a four times better chance of recovery than the child who is spoiled and undisciplined."

Just as a child's obedience or disobedience may determine whether he will recover from an illness, so our attitude in this respect as children of God determines our spiritual health. God says, "This is love, that we walk after His commandments."

If we expect to be blessed by Him, we must obey Him and show forth His love to everyone.

CAUTION

> For many deceivers are entered into the world, who confess not that Jesus Christ is come in the flesh. This is a deceiver and an antichrist. Look to yourselves, that we lose not those things which we have wrought, but that we receive a full reward. Whosoever transgresseth, and abideth not in the doctrine of Christ, hath not God. He that abideth in the doctrine of Christ, he hath both the Father and the Son (2 John 7-9).

As long as the believer walks in love and obeys God, he will enjoy the Lord's blessing. At the same time, he will give convincing evidence of his relationship to his Father in Heaven. There were some in the local churches, however, who did not follow this path. In fact, they forsook the scriptural truth of God's love and "entered into the world" to teach their heretical beliefs. Having given lip service to the truth, they proved themselves to be "deceivers."

The real fallacy as far as these people were concerned was their failure to experience the love of Christ. They flatly denied "that Jesus Christ is come in the flesh." They saw only a human Jesus with no power to save or transform. Denying the incarnation, they left the church and "entered into the world" to spread their pernicious teachings of unbelief.

John cautions all true disciples to keep abounding in

God's love so that they might not succumb to this same error. "Look to yourselves," he says, "that we lose not those things which we have wrought."

The writer of Hebrews tells us of "those who were once enlightened, and have tasted of the heavenly gift, and were made partakers of the Holy Ghost, and have tasted the good word of God, and the powers of the world to come" (Hebrews 6:4-5). This describes the experience of the "deceivers" John writes about. They were so close to the truth, yet so far away. They had received knowledge of God's love as revealed in Christ, but were miles away in unbelief.

Knowledge does not save. One may have knowledge of cancer destroying his body, but unless he submits to available help, he will doubtless die. The same is true of one's spiritual need. Knowing the truth is not sufficient. It must be acted upon through complete submission to Christ.

Thus, warns the apostle, "Look to yourselves"; consider your own life; don't let your efforts for God be in vain; be sure you have received Christ as your Lord. "Examine yourselves, whether ye be in the faith; prove your own selves" (2 Corinthians 13:5).

All of the good works and church going are without meaning unless the Son of God has been received into the life. Those who know Him and faithfully serve Him will never be disappointed, for the day will come when they will "receive a full reward." It will be worth it all when they hear Him say, "Well done, thou good and faithful servant: thou hast been faithful over a few things, I will make thee ruler over many things: enter thou into the joy of thy Lord" (Matthew 25:21).

Often we meet those who say they thought they knew the Lord at one time, but they don't know Him now. Can this be? John says, "Whosoever transgresseth, and abideth not in the doctrine of Christ, hath not God. He that abideth in the doctrine of Christ, he hath both the Father and the Son." John makes it clear that one who really receives the Lord, will *abide* "in the doctrine of Christ." He will not turn away or fall away. We read in Revelation 3:11, "Hold that fast which thou hast, that no man take thy crown." Let there be no question about your own personal salvation. God has made it clear in His Word so that you can know that you are His.

Do you really know that you belong to the Lord? Maybe you are not quite sure. Don't wait any longer; make certain of it immediately. Invite Jesus Christ into your life at this moment and then abide in Him as you grow in grace and mature in the faith.

An insurance company used a question in its advertising, "Can you expect any product to last for a lifetime?" The advertisement proceeded to tell how its company could offer such a product and that in a fast changing and often unpredictable world it is important to have something you can count on.

That's good advice. But even more important is the necessity of providing for security after this life is over. Scripture emphasizes this: "For what is your life? It is even a vapour, that appeareth for a little time, and then vanisheth away" (James 4:14). Have you settled this important issue? Is Jesus Christ your Lord?

INSTRUCTION

> If there come any unto you, and bring not this doctrine,
> receive him not into your house, neither bid him God speed:
> For he that biddeth him God speed is partaker of his evil
> deeds (2 John 10-11).

Having laid the foundation for what he is about to say, John addresses himself to the issue of Christians being hospitable toward those who deny the deity of Christ. Does the commandment we have "from the beginning, that we love one another" apply to our relationships with those who knowingly pervert the Scriptures and teach false doctrine?

The Scriptures speak with clarity relative to the dimensions of the love of Christ which the believer receives by faith. God's love knows no limits of any kind even to the extent of loving those who hate us. Jesus said, "Love your enemies, bless them that curse you, do good to them that hate you, and pray for them which despitefully use you, and persecute you" (Matthew 5:44). The child of God has no liberty at any time to be impolite or discourteous to anyone, even the false teachers.

What then did John mean, "If there come any unto you, and bring not this doctrine, receive him not into your house, neither bid him God speed"?

In the days of the early Church, lodging in homes for

travelers was much more widespread than now. Here and there were a few scattered inns, but they were rarely used by Christians because of the disrepute associated with them. Usually believers sought lodging with other believers along the way.

In John's day opening one's home to traveling evangelists and missionaries was a means of furthering the gospel. "The elect lady" had the obvious problem of those who formerly attended Christian churches, stopping to be entertained after they had openly denied the doctrine of Christ and embraced false teaching. It is against this that John protests. He makes it clear the false teachers were not to be entertained in the homes of Christians since this would only aid them in their attempt to spread heresy. Furthermore, Christians were not in any way given liberty to compromise with unbelief. Unbelief must not be encouraged, but resisted. This is not a denial of the love of God, but an application of it to protect innocent victims from heresy.

It should be realized also that most of the believers in John's day gathered in homes to worship the Lord. There were few buildings built for this purpose only. Though the false teachers were not excluded from worship with believers, whenever they attended they were not to be given any opportunity to speak or teach. They were to have no part in the service. John wrote, "Receive him not into your house, neither bid him God speed." This means that the false teachers were not to be invited to participate in the service and should not in any way be recognized as a friend of the Lord. They were to be treated kindly, but at the same time acknowledged as enemies of the cross.

The danger of giving recognition to the false teachers and allowing them to participate in Christian gatherings is stated clearly: "For he that biddeth him God speed is partaker of his evil deeds." The word partaker as used here means a partner or one who cooperates with another. To show hospitality to a false teacher is to share in his heresy. For a Christian to bid him Godspeed is to participate with him, leaving the impression that the Christian is asking God's blessing on his labors.

The child of God is called upon in the Scriptures to separate himself from anyone or any movement disseminating that which denies the doctrine of Christ. This had become a serious problem among the Corinthian believers. Thus, guided by the Holy Spirit, Paul wrote, "Be ye not unequally yoked together with unbelievers: for what fellowship hath righteousness with unrighteousness? and what communion hath light with darkness? and what concord hath Christ with Belial? or what part hath he that believeth with an infidel? And what agreement hath the temple of God with idols? . . . Wherefore come out from among them, and be ye separate, saith the Lord" (2 Corinthians 6:14-17).

There are many believers in churches who are not satisfied with the liberal preaching they hear week after week. They are doing nothing about it other than complaining. Most of them do not realize that they are living in disobedience to God by supporting such preaching by their attendance and money. Actually they are bidding the liberal preacher "God speed," while becoming partakers of "his evil deeds."

How necessary it is that we who love Christ not only believe the truth but obey it and live for our Saviour without compromise.

ANTICIPATION

Having many things to write unto you, I would not write with paper and ink: but I trust to come unto you, and speak face to face, that our joy may be full. The children of thy elect sister greet thee. Amen (2 John 12-13).

John had spoken of love; now he reveals it as he closes this informal but meaningful Epistle. His parting words give insight into the heart of one who was a man of spiritual depth, fully submitted to Christ.

Having been confronted by false teachers frequently, and well aware of their deceitful and destructive tactics, the apostle might have written an entire epistle giving much detail in warning of their subtle ways. But he was very careful about what he wrote for fear that he might misunderstand and injure a brother in the Lord of whom a false report had been circulated. For this reason he says in tenderness, "Having many things to write unto you, I would not write with paper and ink: but I trust to come unto you, and speak face to face, that our joy may be full."

Probably there was a need for more facts. Sometimes it is difficult to apply a general rule to every situation. John was aware of this. Anticipating his visit with the elect lady and the other saints in her church, he wanted to discuss the matter at length "face to face," or as another translation has it, "heart to heart." He wanted to know who was involved in the heresy. Was he really a heretic or was this mere hearsay? Gossip was a problem in the early church as it is now. John did not want to harm anyone inadvertently.

We must admire this quality. How destructive criticism and gossip has been in the body of Christ. It appears that at times Christians forget who are the real enemies of the cross. Rather than resist false teachers they launch their attack on fellow believers.

The saints of the first church at Jerusalem were guilty of this error. Instead of standing behind Paul and supporting him when he came to their city, they criticized him for what they considered to be carelessness about Jewish regulations. They accused him of lacking in strict orthodoxy. These Christians were so caught up on minor differences that they failed to major on what they could approve.

A critical attitude can cost dearly. Many churches have been hindered severely by critical saints. After all, it is easy to find fault. No training or ability is needed. Just simply overlook the facts. This is what John wanted to avoid. He desired to delay further instruction until he could discuss the issue thoroughly "heart to heart." He knew this procedure would please the Lord. Thus, he preferred to do it this way, as he says, "that our joy may be full."

All sincere believers recognize the blessing of sharing with other believers in an attitude of love while experiencing the joy of fellowship. People of the world gather together for temporary thrills with their alcohol, drugs, and sex. They would laugh uproariously if we were to tell them of our modest times of fellowship together, sharing the things of Christ. But the blind cannot see. The new birth makes the difference. When Christ enters the life, rejoicing with "joy unspeakable and full of glory" becomes an immediate reality (1 Peter 1:8).

A women's meeting had just concluded one afternoon at a fine Bible-believing church in California. About three hundred joyful women were coming out of the church when, providentially, a young woman greatly in need of spiritual help came along. She gazed enviously at the happy faces of the jubilant throng coming from the house of God.

Moments later she found herself entering the church to seek help. The young lady's first words to the pastor were, "I saw all those women coming out of the church and I could tell by their faces that they had something I did not have." After she told the pastor her story of sin and misery, she listened to him unfold the message that produces the joy of the Lord in believers, the good news of salvation through Christ. When he finished, with sincere repentance she opened her heart to the Saviour and experienced the joy she had seen expressed on the faces of the women.

As a further evidence of the joy radiated through Christian love, John bears greetings to the elect lady from "the children" of her "elect sister." Doubtless he had enjoyed the hospitality provided by these friends during a recent mission in the service of Christ.

How wonderful is the fellowship we enjoy as believers, first with Christ, and then with His people as we rejoice in His marvelous love! How gracious of the Lord to make this possible for all who trust in Christ, His Son.

THE THIRD EPISTLE

OF JOHN

3 JOHN

SATISFACTION

The elder unto the wellbeloved Gaius, whom I love in the truth. Beloved, I wish above all things that thou mayest prosper and be in health, even as thy soul prospereth. For I rejoiced greatly, when the brethren came and testified of the truth that is in thee, even as thou walkest in the truth. I have no greater joy than to hear that my children walk in truth (3 John 1-4).

Gaius brought much satisfaction to the heart of the aged Apostle John, for not only was this generous friend well known, he was "wellbeloved." Four times in this letter, John calls him "beloved." Gaius was a humble servant with deep convictions who had proved his worthiness by faithful sacrifice for God.

It is evident that Gaius was not in the best of health. John expresses his concern saying, "I wish above all things that thou mayest prosper and be in health, even as thy soul prospereth." Though weak in body, Gaius was not lacking in soul prosperity. No one would question the fact that good health is a valuable asset. But what about soul prosperity? Is there anything that could provide greater satisfaction on this side of Heaven? To know the Lord and to follow Him consistently in a life of submission is the highest form of living.

My wife and I have a dear friend who, though in her thirties, is only twenty-three inches tall. Her hip and ankle bones are dislocated and she suffers from numerous other complications. Her body cannot tolerate solid foods so she lives on strained foods and liquids. One might expect to hear her complain on occasion, but never. She has a sweet spirit and is unusually concerned about the welfare of others. This young lady lives in a frail body but she is well known for her great faith and peaceful composure. Her body did not mature as other adults' did but her soul has prospered in a remarkable way. It is refreshing to be in her presence; her letters abound with praise to the Lord.

We are not told what Gaius's illness was, but more importantly we are assured from the Word that he prospered in soul. Friends kept John informed of his persistent growth in grace and fruitful service. Not only did Gaius know "the truth," but he walked "in the truth." To walk in the truth is to live in obedience to the will of God.

When the apostle received this good news about Gaius, he "rejoiced greatly," giving thanks to the Lord. John had learned over the years that living in God's will was the only way of blessing. Like David, he could say, "I delight to do Thy will, O my God" (Psalm 40:8). When one seeks above all else to obey God and do His will, he will surely discover untold enjoyment.

It appears that Gaius came to know Christ under John's ministry. This too brought satisfaction to the heart of the apostle. He wrote, "I have no greater joy than to hear that my children walk in truth." It is thrilling to be used of the Lord to lead others to Christ, but to watch them grow and mature in the faith is an added delight.

We cannot help to be concerned when we consider the vast number of believers who have never once attempted to lead an unsaved person to Christ. What satisfaction they are missing.

I shall never forget the night when God gave me the privilege of leading my first soul to Christ, shortly after I was saved. It was such an extraordinary experience that I was unable to get to sleep until early the next morning. The thrill continues as I share the message of grace with the unsaved and see needy hearts turn to Christ.

Can you imagine the joy that will be ours when we meet people in Heaven who are there because we cared enough to tell them about the Lord Jesus? Talk about "joy unspeakable and full of glory"; that will be it. This being true, we ought to grasp every opportunity to tell others about our Lord.

Following her conversion, a teenager asked God for the courage to share her faith with every one of the one hundred and fifty students in her school on a one-to-one basis. God granted this request and, as the result, fifteen of her fellow students were saved.

Suppose all believers were witnessing in a similar manner. Who could begin to estimate the results? God has called us to share the truth. He says, "Ye are My witnesses" (Isaiah 43:12). Let's tell others about the Lord Jesus and enjoy the blessing.

COMMENDATION

Beloved, thou doest faithfully whatsoever thou doest to the brethren, and to strangers; Which have borne witness of thy charity before the church: whom if thou bring forward on their journey after a godly sort, thou shalt do well: Because that for His name's sake they went forth, taking nothing of the Gentiles. We therefore ought to receive such, that we might be fellowhelpers to the truth (3 John 5-8).

Gaius was a zealous saint with a heart for the lost. But he was also a kind and benevolent gentleman who was well known for his hospitality to traveling missionaries and evangelists. He was always ready and willing to open the door of his home to God's servants and to make them as relaxed and comfortable as possible.

John commended Gaius for this highly worthwhile and sacrificial service which was not only costly but time consuming. "Beloved, thou doest faithfully whatsoever thou doest to the brethren, and to strangers."

Among the regular guests who stopped for food and lodging at Gaius's house were strangers. They were not strangers for long, however, for Gaius was quick to befriend them with Christian love and thoughtfulness.

Those who had been entertained by Gaius did not soon forget his loving kindness. As they traveled from town to town preaching and teaching the Word in the various churches, they told of God's gracious servant who was performing this unusual ministry: they "have borne witness of thy charity before the church."

Further insight is given into the gracious service of Gaius: "Whom if thou bring forward on their journey after a godly sort, thou shalt do well." Not only did Gaius care for the needs of the travelers while they were guests in his home, but when they were ready to leave he went with them a short way to be sure they got started on the right road. There was just no limit to the extent of this man's consideration for others.

Traveling in John's day was extremely difficult and hazardous. With conditions as they were, we might wonder why so many Christians were on the roads. John tells us why. "Because that for His name's sake they went forth." They were giving of themselves and all they had for the glory of God, "for His name's sake." Having come to know the Lord Jesus, they dedicated themselves to the ministry of sharing the blessed gospel with thousands who had never heard. What Jesus said in Mark 16:15 was very meaningful to them, "Go ye into all the world, and preach the gospel to every creature." They accepted the challenge and acted upon it.

James Leonard Hansberry, the last survivor of Dr. Walter Reed's yellow fever experiments in 1901, died several years ago. Dr. Reed proved that the scourge of yellow fever was carried by mosquitoes. A subsequent vaccine virtually eliminated the possibility of contracting this usually fatal disease that had become a killer in many parts of the world.

Mr. Hansberry was a private in the United States Army at the time he volunteered to help in the experiment. He was exposed to mosquito bites, contracted the disease, and nearly died. His life was spared, however, and he obtained a $300 reward and a $200-a-month life pension. When asked why he risked his life by volunteering, he gave the simple reply, "It was the thing to do." Millions were perishing with yellow fever. Mr. Hansberry refused to stand by and do nothing. For him, "it was the thing to do."

Most of those who accepted hospitality in Gaius's home were motivated by a similar concern. There were many thousands perishing without Christ who needed to hear the gospel. Regardless of the hazards these dedicated volunteers "went every where preaching the word" (Acts 8:4). They left their employment, their families, and their security to propagate the truth.

Few of these roving witnesses were in a position to support themselves. In most cases, when they departed from their homes their income ceased. Theirs was strictly a work of faith. They were dependent totally upon God's merciful provision through His people. Regardless of how pressing their needs were they refused to go to the unsaved for help, lest they might be accused of commercialization: "They went forth, taking nothing of the Gentiles."

John commends Gaius again for his worthy ministry, stressing the fact that all believers ought to follow his splendid example and open their homes to the ambassadors of the cross, "We therefore ought to receive such." In so doing, not only were the needy travelers helped, but the hosts shared the blessing of spreading the gospel, "That we might be fellowhelpers to the truth."

Not all of us have the gift of preaching and teaching, but every believer has a gift or gifts. Gaius, like many in our day, might have excused himself from active service since he could not travel about to make Christ known. We are not told what his reasons were; possibly health, age, or family responsibilities. Nevertheless, he was not willing to give up that easily. He realized that worldwide evangelization was every believer's responsibility and he dared to exercise his gift of "helps" to do his best for the Lord.

OPPOSITION

> I wrote unto the church: but Diotrephes, who loveth to have the preeminence among them, receiveth us not. Wherefore, if I come, I will remember his deeds which he doeth, prating against us with malicious words: and not content therewith, neither doth he himself receive the brethren, and forbiddeth them that would, and casteth them out of the church (3 John 9-10).

Wherever the Lord is doing a work, it is certain that the devil will appear on the scene to oppose all that is good. This was true in the case of Gaius. It seems that he attended the same church as a man by the name of Diotrephes, who was extremely proud. Because of his intellectual ability Diotrephes was well received by some in the congregation. He would have nothing to do with Gaius or any of his guests. Furthermore, he had little respect for John's position as an apostle and elder, and practically ignored all his communications. John says,

"I wrote unto the church: but Diotrephes, who loveth to have the preeminence among them, receiveth us not."

Diotrephes may have even been the pastor of the church. If he was not the pastor, it is obvious that he was an officer who had acquired much authority. Acting in the flesh, he had no regard for the guidance of the Holy Spirit. Likewise, he had no interest in the Scriptural qualifications for church leadership.

Peter exhorts those who are responsible for leadership in the church to "feed the flock of God which is among you." Then he adds, "Neither as being lords over God's heritage, but being ensamples to the flock" (1 Peter 5:2-3).

Regrettably, like Diotrephes many in our day have assumed powers and authority that God never intended. Rather than preach and teach the Word in the power of the Holy Spirit, they have become "lords over God's heritage" and have sought to explain the Scriptures to their own personal advantage.

Diotrephes refused to allow anyone to speak or teach in the church who was in any way favorable toward Gaius or John. Obviously he excluded these people fearing they would be a threat to his leadership. Those visiting with Gaius were often Spirit-filled men of God who were being used of the Lord to reach the lost for Christ. They had seen God at work performing miracles in lives and homes. Were they to speak in the presence of Diotrephes the hearers would have easily recognized the superiority of their Spirit-directed teaching as opposed to Diotrephes's intellectual approach. Diotrephes was afraid of this and took careful precaution so that it could not happen.

The Apostle John was greatly disturbed by this

selfish attitude on the part of Diotrephes: "Wherefore, if I come, I will remember his deeds which he doeth." It was doubtful that the aged apostle with failing health would be making the journey, but he certainly coveted the opportunity. Diotrephes needed to be confronted and instructed from the Scriptures relative to his "prating" and "malicious words."

In an attempt to justify himself, Diotrephes had been spreading malicious reports about John and Gaius and their friends. Selfishly he was exalting himself while attempting to ruin the character of anyone who did not support him. He was so intent upon accomplishing his own evil purposes that if anyone disagreed with him, John says that he "casteth them out of the church."

Unfortunately the Diotrephes spirit has continued down through the ages resulting in divided congregations, church splits, and thousands of wounded lives. Rarely are church problems doctrinal. Usually they are instigated by selfish individuals like Diotrephes. Often Scripture is used as a cloak, but the basic cause is the pride of selfish hearts.

When Bob Feller was only seventeen years of age he was signed to play big league baseball. The trainer for the Cleveland Indians happened to be present when young Robert first tried on his new uniform.

"Well, son," the old-timer asked, "how does it fit?"

Nervously putting on his new cap and sliding it around on his head, the young man replied, "The cap seems a little big."

The trainer came back quickly with, "See that it stays that way."

That was good advice. How essential that each believer permits the Holy Spirit to deal with the evil of pride on a daily basis, for "pride goeth before destruction, and an haughty spirit before a fall" (Proverbs 16:18). Many of God's people have destroyed their usefulness and fallen into disrepute simply because they failed to allow the Lord to give victory over pride.

APPLICATION

Beloved, follow not that which is evil, but that which is good. He that doeth good is of God: but he that doeth evil hath not seen God. Demetrius hath good report of all men, and of the truth itself: yea, and we also bear record; and ye know that our record is true. I had many things to write, but I will not with ink and pen write unto thee: but I trust I shall shortly see thee, and we shall speak face to face. Peace be to thee. Our friends salute thee. Greet the friends by name (3 John 11-14).

What the apostle has written might easily be read hastily with little thought. But John is concerned that we get hold of the contents and apply them to our own lives. "Beloved, follow not that which is evil, but that which is good." We have seen the good traits of love and generosity exemplified in Gaius. On the other hand we have seen the evil traits of pride and selfishness in the life of Diotrephes. John urges us not to imitate the evil but the good. If we imitate the good this is a favorable indication that we belong to the Lord. If we follow the way of evil our relationship to Christ is dubious.

All of us are prone to imitate. We begin in childhood

and continue until death. It isn't long until the little toddler begins to imitate many of the characteristics of his mother and dad. Later, after starting to school, he absorbs many of the traits of other children. This process continues and never ceases. Regrettably, it seems that most people are more prone to imitate the evil rather than the good. Only Christ can make the difference. As daily we submit to His loving control and leadership, He gives the enablement to turn from the evil to follow the good.

John at this point introduces us to another friend: "Demetrius hath good report of all men, and of the truth itself: yea, and we also bear record; and ye know that our record is true."

Who was Demetrius? Little is known of this servant of Christ other than that he was a sincere saint of whom God's people spoke very highly. Possibly he had been one of the faithful members of the same fellowship as Gaius. As the result of his consistent witness he was expelled from the church by the proud Diotrephes, who considered Demetrius also to be a hindrance to his authority and leadership.

Whoever Demetrius was, it is evident that someone had sought to malign his character. John was quick to come to his defense. The apostle knew it would be sinful to be silent when a Christian brother like Demetrius was being accused falsely. God's people are one in the fellowship of the Body of Christ. Each is part of the other and should not remain idle when a brother in Christ needs help: With love, God's people must stand for each other in the face of evil.

John concludes this Epistle as he did his previous one: "I had many things to write, but I will not with ink and pen write unto thee: but I trust I shall shortly see thee, and we shall speak face to face." There were many things yet to be said about Diotrephes and what was happening in the church. It was better, however, that this wait until the next face-to-face meeting. It is usually preferable to discuss things verbally rather than by letter.

Every believer should be looking forward to the greatest face-to-face meeting of all time. What a glorious day it will be when we are "caught up . . . to meet the Lord in the air" to be with Him forever (1 Thessalonians 4:17). Sorrow and separation will be destroyed by the blessed presence of the Lord Jesus when we see Him face to face. Have you ever taken the time to sit down, close your eyes, and try to visualize what that meeting will be like? Try it! Do it often! It will rekindle the fire in your heart.

"Peace be to thee." We don't have the visible presence of Christ yet, but we are assured of His present peace. He says, "Peace I leave with you, My peace I give unto you" (John 14:27). Christ's peace cannot compare with His presence but He desires that we enjoy His peace until we are with Him. Are you enjoying it? Do you have His peace in your life? Maybe you have never really received Him as your Saviour and Lord. You may have knowledge of Him, and believe in Him, but have you actually received Him? If not, do it now, the best way you know how, so you will be ready to meet Him when He comes.

For his closing remarks John bears greetings from mutual friends. Likewise he desires to be remembered to his many friends residing near Gaius, as well as the faithful ones passing through his home. How marvelous is the fellowship of the saints! What a blessed privilege it is to be a member of the Body of Christ!